Never Make an Uninformed Financial Decision Again

Book 4: Now You Have Money

and

Book 5: Money for Fun

by Hayden Burrus

Text copyright © Hayden Burrus

All Rights Reserved

Table of Contents

Book 4 – Now You Have Money 3

- Chapter 1 - Bad Lines of Credit 4
- Chapter 2 - Borrowing for Grownups and Mortgages 7
- Chapter 3 - What Would You Do If You Had $100,000 18
- Chapter 4 - Investing for Grownups 21
- Chapter 5 - Roth or not Roth 28
- Chapter 6 - IRA issues 32
- Chapter 7 - Time to Sell the House 43
- Chapter 8 - Writing a Will 48
- Chapter 9 - Talking Money with Your Adult Kids 56
- Chapter 10 - Talking Money with Your Parents 59
- Chapter 11 - A Whole Chapter on Life insurance and Annuities 64
- Chapter 12 - Annuities 75
- Chapter 13 - I'm Going to Open My Own Business 82
- Chapter 14 - First Steps for Aspiring Business Owners 87
- Chapter 15 - Combining Finances with Your Significant Other 93

Book 5 – Extra Credit – Money for Fun 96
    Chapter 1 - What Would You Do if You Had $1,000,000 97
    Chapter 2 - Lending 104
    Chapter 3 - Set for Life..111
    Chapter 4 - What Would You Do If You Won the Lottery?..117
    Chapter 5 - How Do You Rate? 124
    Chapter 6 - Investing Personalities 130
    Chapter 7 - Sources of Investing Information......139
    Chapter 8 - Cautionary Tales 145
    Chapter 9 - Charity..148
    Chapter 10 - An Inspiring Tale - Rags to Riches.156

Book 4 – Now You Have Money

Chapter 1 - Bad Lines of Credit

A line of credit is an account given to you by a financial institution where you can borrow any amount of money up to the credit limit at any time. You can also pay back the loan in full or in part according to your own schedule (subject to the minimum payment requirements). All things being equal, it's way better than a regular loan because of its flexibility. You are 100% in control of both the inflows and outflows of the loan.

A credit card is a line of credit, albeit a bad one because of the very high interest rates (between 19% and 29% per year). The only good thing about using a credit card for your line of credit is that credit cards are very easy to get. When I was in college, everyone, even the basket weaving majors, could get a credit card with a $5,000 credit line. Credit cards are most people's entry into lines of credit. Ideally you want to keep a credit card with no annual fee in reserve. Don't charge on it, just keep it as a backup in case you are really up against the wall with spending needs and your emergency fund can't pay the expense. Remember: a credit card with a zero balance is a backup emergency fund, a credit card with a balance on it is a ticket to the poor house.

Overdraft protection provided by your bank is another type of line of credit. Overdraft protection is linked to your checking account. If you write a check or make an ATM withdrawal that exceeds your bank balance, the overdraft protection will kick in. Your bank will transfer money from your overdraft protection line of credit to your checking account and allow the check to go through. They then add a fee and they start charging you interest. They also apply any deposits you make to the line of credit before they allow your balance to rise above $0 again. As long as your account is below $0, they are charging fees ($15 to $35) for every transaction and it adds up really fast.

If you aren't careful, the bank fees-- potentially $100s per month can keep your bank balance at $0 for a long time. On the other hand it does save you the embarrassment, hassle, and fees associated with bounced checks. If you use your bank account for lots of little transactions and very few large transactions, you may wish to decline overdraft protection even if it's free. The typical person in the real world ends up using overdraft protection by accident rather than on purpose. He uses it because he lost track of his balance, maybe because a deposit didn't go through or he forgot about a large check he wrote earlier in the month. The first transaction leading to his account balance dropping below $0 will result in a $35 overdraft protection fee. This fee may be worth it as it prevents the bounced check fees that your payee charges. For your "convenience", the overdraft protection (and fee) is applied automatically, without even notifying you. This convenience results in your going about your day without even knowing you are overdrawn. If you are the type of person who may make several check or debit card purchases a day, this could be a disaster. The next time you use your debit card to buy a candy bar, your candy bar will be costing you $36 rather than $1 because of the overdraft fee. You won't even find out that your candy bar was $36 until the next time you look at your bank statement. If you are like many people, you may make ten or more debit card purchases before the next time you look at your bank balance. Hopefully you are able to deposit the money you are overdrawn before the end of the day or the overdraft protection fees will stick permanently. Personally, I'd rather bounce a check and be embarrassed once, and pay $50 or so in bounced check charges than pay $350 in overdraft fees. If you are like the typical person described above, you may wish to consider declining the "free" overdraft protection. If you are really on top of your spending and watch your bank balance, then you can go ahead and sign up. You'll be in a position to avoid the overdraft fees. Of course if you are really on top of your spending and watch your bank balance, you'll never use the overdraft protection. This is the only way for you to get what you pay for with an overdraft line of credit.

Chapter 2 - Borrowing for Grownups and Mortgages

A mortgage is pretty much the cheapest way to borrow money for the long term. Borrowing rates for mortgages have always been only a point or so above the long term borrowing rates the US government enjoys with its 30 year bond. And mortgages have a kicker-- if interest rates go down or your financial situation changes you can refinance or pay off your mortgage early no questions asked, without penalty.

If you shop around, have good credit, and have a down payment of 20%, you can now get a mortgage in the high 2% range!! That's just too amazing. When I was a kid mortgages were well over 10%. When I was a teenager, my mother was proud to get her first mortgage for only 8%. My first mortgage on my house was an amazingly great deal—I negotiated down to 7.3%.

Today you can get a mortgage about 70% more cheaply than you could 30 years ago. Not many things have dropped in price by 70% or more over the past 30 years (long distance phone calls and electronics are the only 2 things I can think of). So don't expect rates to go down from here. Looking a few years into the future, I think rates will be higher.

So if you are looking for a mortgage in this environment (2017) almost certainly you should be looking at a fixed mortgage. If you view your home as a starter home that you are only staying with for a few years, you may want to consider a 7/1 ARM (ARM = Adjustable Rate Mortgage). These mortgages have a lower rate, but if you keep them for longer than seven years, they will adjust to current interest rates each year. Rates will likely be higher then. When rates rise, so does your mortgage payment.

I wouldn't choose a fixed period less than seven years. The savings on 5/1 ARMs and 3/1 ARMs are miniscule. On my review of current rates, a $1000 monthly payment for a 7/1 ARM will drop by only $32 if you go with a 3/1 ARM. If you stick with a 3/1 ARM and short term rates rise to 4.5% in three years, your monthly payment will rise by $220. The cost of the potential monthly payment increase for the remaining 27 years of your mortgage far outweighs the benefit of the lower monthly payments for the first few years of your mortgage. Make sure you choose a mortgage with a fixed term that is the longest you can reasonably expect to have your home for. I plan to live in my home for life so I rejected all ARMs and went with a fixed rate mortgage.

Now, if you are only going to be in the home for a few years, it is probably not worth it to buy. Keep renting. If you buy, your non-refundable mortgage fees are going to run you about $6,000 to $7,000 on a $250K mortgage. If you have to pay a broker's commission on top of that, your non refundable costs can come out to about $400 per month if you are in the house for 36 months. This more than offsets the savings from home ownership.

Finally, you want to figure out the right time period for the mortgage to be paid back. Here you have some flexibility. If you can afford it, you want to shoot for a shorter term. As an example, currently 15 year mortgages have interest rates about 1.0% lower than 30 year mortgages. As a result the total payments over the life of the mortgage are almost 30% less if you choose the 15 year term. Monthly payments, however, are about 50% more. If you can't afford these higher payments, it is probably OK to stick with a 30 year term if you are reasonably young and the 30 year term can allow you to increase your retirement fund contributions.

Yes, it is just **probably** OK to go with the 30 year mortgage. The longest time period your mortgage should last is from now until the date you retire. So for those of us older than about 35, we should be exploring a shorter term mortgage. You'll be able to afford this shorter term mortgage because you (hopefully) have saved up some money by the time you are 35, will be getting a lower interest rate, and are also making more money than you did a few years ago. Even if that is not true, you need to make sure that your mortgage is gone by the time you retire.

Once you know what you are looking for, you can work on getting the best deal.

At a high level, here are the things you need to be looking at when you do your comparison shopping:

- The terms (how many years fixed, how does it adjust).
- The points and origination fees (this is essentially the commission that your friendly mortgage broker is getting).
- All of the other expenses – these should be pretty similar between mortgages, but sometimes they aren't. Here's where some unscrupulous brokers siphon off a little more of your money for themselves.
- And of course, the interest rate.

You need to be paying attention to all of these things. Some mortgages can look very attractive when looking at just one of these items (e.g. the interest rate), but look awful when looking at the other items.

Now there are lots of good ways to select the best available mortgage. However many of them are quite complicated. Rather than introducing you to elementary financial theory and the concepts of net present value and internal rate of return, I'll just tell you the story of how I got my mortgage.

First off, I did not go to a bank. Banks are the worst place to get a mortgage. The bigger the bank, the worse deal they will have available for a mortgage. For fun I recently compared the best rate from a big bank to the best rate I could quickly find for a 30 year fixed mortgage with zero points. The monthly payment for the big bank mortgage is $55 per month more for a $250K loan. Multiply that by 360 months and you get to about $21K in extra payments to the big bank. Don't do that.

I did all of my mortgage shopping on the web. I went to a site called bankrate.com. There are other good sites out there too, just search "cheapest mortgage" or something like that. Anyway, Bankrate lets you choose the type of mortgage you are interested in right on the home screen. I selected 15 year fixed (I am over 40 years old). Then, when the list popped up, I immediately chose to sort by interest rate. Next, I picked up the phone and dialed the lenders offering the five best interest rates.

The reason why I called five lenders instead of just the best one is that sometimes the fees and expenses are significantly different between lenders. Also, sometimes a lender will end up offering you a different interest rate (higher or lower) from what was advertised. They do this based on specific information they learn from you during the application process. This part is a real hassle. You might be on the phone with each lender for about 30 minutes each. It's worth it, though, because the difference between a great mortgage and a good mortgage over the lifespan of the loan is potentially tens of thousands of dollars. I don't know about you, but I am willing to spend a half day's effort to save that kind of money on mortgage costs.

During this part, take great notes. Know the phone # you dialed, the people you talked to, the promises they made, and the additional information they asked for from you. Most lenders eventually send a "Uniform Residential Loan Application" to you with your information already filled in. Look this over closely and correct any errors. The lender will use this information to run a credit report (which you pay for) and prepare a Good Faith Estimate (GFE). Make sure all the promises the mortgage lenders made are on the GFE. If the promises aren't in writing, then they will not be honored. You will not have to pay any other fees prior to getting a good faith estimate.

Before you go any further, make sure you chose loan terms that suit your needs. The Good Faith Estimate (GFE) lists the terms and costs of the loan. Here's where the lender "puts their money where their mouth is". They are making a promise that, if you go through with the application, and they approve the loan, their terms and expenses will be essentially identical to the GFE. The GFE is on a standard form produced by HUD. This will allow you to easily compare GFEs between lenders.

OMB Approval No. 2502-0265

Good Faith Estimate (GFE)

Name of Originator	Borrower
Originator Address	Property Address
Originator Phone Number	
Originator Email	Date of GFE

Purpose — This GFE gives you an estimate of your settlement charges and loan terms if you are approved for this loan. For more information, see HUD's Special Information Booklet on settlement charges, your *Truth-in-Lending Disclosures*, and other consumer information at www.hud.gov/respa. If you decide you would like to proceed with this loan, contact us.

Shopping for your loan — Only you can shop for the best loan for you. Compare this GFE with other loan offers, so you can find the best loan. Use the shopping chart on page 3 to compare all the offers you receive.

Important dates

1. The interest rate for this GFE is available through [_____]. After this time, the interest rate, some of your loan Origination Charges, and the monthly payment shown below can change until you lock your interest rate.
2. This estimate for all other settlement charges is available through [__3__].
3. After you lock your interest rate, you must go to settlement within [30] days (your rate lock period) to receive the locked interest rate.
4. You must lock the interest rate at least [0] days before settlement.

Summary of your loan

Your initial loan amount is	$
Your loan term is	15 years
Your initial interest rate is	3.000 %
Your initial monthly amount owed for principal, interest, and any mortgage insurance is	$ per month
Can your interest rate rise?	[X] No [ ] Yes, it can rise to a maximum of ___%. The first change will be in ___.
Even if you make payments on time, can your loan balance rise?	[X] No [ ] Yes, it can rise to a maximum of $___.
Even if you make payments on time, can your monthly amount owed for principal, interest, and any mortgage insurance rise?	[X] No [ ] Yes, the first increase can be in ___ and the monthly amount owed can rise to $___. The maximum it can ever rise to is $___.
Does your loan have a prepayment penalty?	[X] No [ ] Yes, your maximum prepayment penalty is $___.
Does your loan have a balloon payment?	[X] No [ ] Yes, you have a balloon payment of $___ due in ___ years.

Escrow account information — Some lenders require an escrow account to hold funds for paying property taxes or other property-related charges in addition to your monthly amount owed of $[____].
Do we require you to have an escrow account for your loan?
[X] No, you do not have an escrow account. You must pay these charges directly when due.
[ ] Yes, you have an escrow account. It may or may not cover all of these charges. Ask us.

Summary of your settlement charges

A	Your Adjusted Origination Charges *(See page 2.)*	$	2,534.60
B	Your Charges for All Other Settlement Services *(See page 2.)*	$	5,541.98
A + B	Total Estimated Settlement Charges	$	8,076.58

GFE p1 (eff. Jan 2010) ~ 04/2011 ~ Encompass360®

Understanding your estimated settlement charges

Your Adjusted Origination Charges

1. Our origination charge This charge is for getting this loan for you.	1,995.00
2. Your credit or charge (points) for the specific interest rate chosen ☐ The credit or charge for the interest rate of [____] % is included in "Our origination charge." (See item 1 above.) ☐ You receive a credit of $[____] for this interest rate of [____] %. This credit **reduces** your settlement charges. ☒ You pay a charge of $ **539.60** for this interest rate of **3.000** %. This charge (points) **increases** your total settlement charges. The tradeoff table on page 3 shows that you can change your total settlement charges by choosing a different interest rate for this loan.	539.60
A **Your Adjusted Origination Charges**	$ 2,534.60

Your Charges for All Other Settlement Services

Some of these charges can change at settlement. See the top of page 3 for more information.

3. Required services that we select — 478.25

These charges are for services we require to complete your settlement. We will choose the providers of these services.

Service	Charge	Service	Charge
Appraisal Fee	395.00		
Credit Report	16.75		
Tax Service	61.00		
Flood Certification	5.50		

4. Title services and lender's title insurance — 2,028.00
This charge includes the services of a title or settlement agent, for example, and title insurance to protect the lender, if required.

5. Owner's title insurance
You may purchase an owner's title insurance policy to protect your interest in the property.

6. Required services that you can shop for — 0.00
These charges are for other services that are required to complete your settlement. We can identify providers of these services or you can shop for them yourself. Our estimates for providing these services are below.

Service	Charge	Service	Charge

7. Government recording charges — 216.70
These charges are for state and local fees to record your loan and title documents.

8. Transfer taxes — 2,090.70
These charges are for state and local fees on mortgages and home sales.

9. Initial deposit for your escrow account — 0.00
This charge is held in an escrow account to pay future recurring charges on your property and includes ☐ all property taxes, ☐ all insurance, and ☐ other [____]

10. Daily interest charges — 728.33
This charge is for the daily interest on your loan from the day of your settlement until the first day of the next month or the first day of your normal mortgage payment cycle. This amount is $ **31.6667** per day for **23** days (if your settlement is **12/09/2013**).

11. Homeowner's insurance — 0.00
This charge is for the insurance you must buy for the property to protect from a loss, such as fire.

Policy	Charge

B Your Charges for All Other Settlement	$	5,541.98
A + **B** Total Estimated Settlement Charges	$	8,076.58

 Good Faith Estimate (HUD-GFE) 2

Page 1 of the GFE has summary information. Look at this first. Look at the loan amount, term, interest rate, and the answer to the question "Can your interest rate rise?" These items should be exactly the same as what the loan officer explained to you over the phone. Your goal here is to have all of the above mentioned items identical for each of the GFE's you are getting. This will make your comparison shopping easier. Your loan will follow the GFE, not some promise or email written by a loan officer. If they are different, don't go any further. Call back the lender and get the lender to explain or correct the misunderstanding in writing. For now, you can skip the initial monthly payment part.

Next, move on to page 2. The key parts to page 2 of the GFE are items #1, #2, #3, and #4. Add these items up. This dollar amount is the payments you will make that is in the control of the mortgage broker / lender. The first two are direct payments to the lender, and the next two are for payments to the lender's affiliates. This is money deducted from your loan, money out of your pocket. All things being equal, choose the lender with the lowest total cost for these items. Great! Now you've got your lender.

Remember: Once you have selected your lender, call your loan officer; explain you want to move forward; and tell the officer you want to lock in the interest rate for your loan for at least 45 days.

The last thing you want is a nasty surprise at closing where you find out that your new interest rate and loan payment is higher than what you thought it would be because you didn't lock in the loan.

Here I'll take a break to talk about all the items that I skipped over and didn't tell you to pay attention to. First, the monthly payment! Yes, I skipped that on purpose. Here's why—The monthly payment may be calculated to include a payment for your property tax, homeowners dues, and property insurance. Different lenders may make different estimates for these items. The lender's estimate does not matter, because if they estimate low, you just have to make up the difference. An unscrupulous lender may low-ball these items in order to make the cost of your loan appear lower. Don't fall for it. Ignore this section.

Next, the GFE displays several different additional expenses on rows 5 to 11. These items are estimates. #6 and #11 are in your control, and therefore the lender's estimate doesn't matter. #7 and #8 are tax payments that will be the same regardless of your lender.

#9 and #10 are in the lender's control. However these items do not influence your total costs. These items just influence whether or not you pay these costs at the time you get the loan. For example #9 is the initial deposit on your escrow account. This item is $0.00 on my GFE. This just means that I am not giving any money to the lender to pay for insurance and taxes on my behalf. I still have to pay these bills when they come due. I prefer to hold my money and be in charge of my own bill paying. The lender agreed and put a $0 charge for #9.

#10 is advance payments you are making for the interest on your mortgage between the day the mortgage closes and your first mortgage payment. In my GFE the payment is calculated to be $728.33

because the mortgage in this example was estimated to settle on 12/9/2013, and the first loan payment was not due until 2/1/2014. This number can be manipulated by the lender choosing a different settlement date. For example, if the lender chose a settlement date of 2/1/2014 there would be no interest charges, but I would have to make my first loan payment right away. #10 reflects a tradeoff between getting your mortgage money sooner and reducing your closing cost. It does not reflect a true cost.

Chapter 3 - What Would You Do If You Had $100,000

Getting a windfall of $100K is exciting. It's also quite likely over the long term if you make good saving and investing decisions. This first thing to do when looking at a six figure net worth is to make sure that you've got your financial foundation covered. $100K - now you can do whatever you want-- party, buy a car, vacation in Tahiti. Or... you can take $100 spend it on a fun but not extravagant Friday night, and invest the rest. It may sound boring. Many of my financially challenged friends would respond to that idea with "what good is money if you can't ever enjoy it?", or "how can $100K in the bank make me happy?" Here's how:

$100K properly invested can provide you with about $7K per year in income forever. Not the rest of your life, but for the rest of the lives of all of your descendants all the way until the world comes to an end. If you want this income to increase with inflation (which you should), you would still be able to draw about $4K per year-- that's about $75/week, forever. That's Friday night drinks, forever.

You may feel you don't need an extra $75/week right now. Great! Invest it for retirement. Investment dollars double every 7 to 10 years. So, if you are young enough, you should get 4 or maybe five doubles before you retire. $2 \times 2 \times 2 \times 2 = 16x$ (4 doubles -- 28 to 40 years investing) $2 \times 2 \times 2 \times 2 \times 2 = 32x$ (5 doubles-- 35 to 50 years investing). At retirement, your money will have grown to somewhere between $1,600K and 3,200K. Your investment money will now be able to generate somewhere between $64K and $128K per year, forever ($20K to $50K per year in today's $).

Interestingly, I actually lived through a similar scenario in my younger years. My mother passed away and I inherited about $50K after expenses. That's about $100K in today's dollars. I wasn't a financial coach back then. However I was naturally skilled in managing my personal finances. Once all of the medical and funeral expenses settled, and after her possessions and investments were transferred to me (I was the sole heir), I was able to see that I had received about $50K. I checked my student loan debt balance. It was $10K. I wrote a check and paid it off.

I had $40K left. I was planning on purchasing a house in the near future and the houses I was looking at required a $30K down payment (people put 20% down at that time). I figured that I would need another $10K or so for repairs, fixups, and new furniture (most of my furniture were hand me downs or college furniture). I put the $40K in the bank. No party for me. I was happy with my decision, though. The next step in my financial life was falling into place.

Six months later I bought a fixer-upper house and put $29K down. The first year into the house I spent the remaining $11K on repairs and to replace furniture that my girlfriend made me throw out. I still live in that now fixed up house today (20 years later).

Me, I'll go for investing the money rather than 3-6 months of partying.

Chapter 4 - Investing for Grownups

This chapter is not at the beginning of the book for good reason. A big part of your personal and financial life has to come together before you should even think of starting down the road as an investor. You must fulfill all of the conditions below to start your investing life:

- Steady income greater than expenses.
- No debt charging interest more than 4% over the interest earned on a high interest savings account (currently about 1.0%).
- Emergency fund with greater than three months living expenses in high interest savings account.
- Contributing as much as you need to your company retirement plan in order to be awarded the maximum employer match on retirement contributions. Usually this happens when you contribute 6% of your income.
- Additional savings that can pay for all major expenses (more than one month's living expenses) expected in the next year.
- Additional savings towards all major expenses due in the next five years.

That's a pretty heavy duty list! Some people meet all of these conditions within a year or two after they get their first full time job. For others it can take ten years or more even if they are doing all of the right things. Some people never get there (but it usually means they aren't handling their finances correctly in the first place). The point is this-- you need a rock solid financial foundation that can address all of your day to day and even year-to-year needs before you get started investing.

Investing is for the long term. And I mean looooong term-- many years, decades, to retirement, and beyond. The reason why you need to think long term is that investments, even good investments, can lose value for a very long period of time. The stock market decreases in value about one out of every three years. It can be three, five, even seven years from the time the stock market starts going down until it bottoms out and then rises back to even. If you need to draw out your money in a shorter amount of time, you might find that not all of the money you invested is still there.

If you invest in individual stocks, the potential for major stock market declines and waiting a long time until recovery is even greater. Take Amazon, a great investment and a great company according to pretty much everyone. In 1999 its price was over $300 per share. In the next few years it lost over 95% of its value. The price didn't reach $300 again until 2013. If you had invested in Amazon in 1999, you would have had to wait fourteen years (if you could wait that long) to see even a penny of return. And that's a great investment.

Good investments are more likely to go up than down in the long term. And when they go up, they increase more than they decrease. However with investing, especially in the short and medium term, you just don't know. So that's why you shouldn't invest any money that you are going to be needing any time soon.

Unless you are starting out with millions of dollars, you definitely don't need an investment adviser to start. You can do this on your own. Actually, you <u>should</u> do this on your own because your investment costs will almost certainly be lower, and your investment returns will probably be better. Type "percentage of mutual funds that beat the S&P 500" into your favorite search engine. There are always dozens of research articles calculating the chances of an "actively managed fund" sold by an adviser beating the S&P 500 stock market index. At the time of this writing the articles I find that between 66% and 86% of all of these adviser recommended funds have lower returns than the S&P 500. That means **66% to 86% are worse than a stock market index you can buy yourself without any broker or "financial adviser" at all.** I'll take those odds.

So if you want your investments to perform better than 66% to 86% of the "financial advisers" out there you'll find a way to invest in the stock market index. Fortunately there are several good fund companies that have mutual funds that do exactly that. Vanguard, Fidelity, Schwab, Blackrock are four big great reputable names that have low cost S&P500 funds; there are many other great ones as well. They all have an online presence and people you can reach by phone to help you fill out paperwork to open an account. Be sure to choose the SP500 index fund investment. Send in your check. Now you are an investor that will beat 66% to 86% of the investment professionals out there.

Where do you send in your check? You need to send in your check to an <u>investment custodian</u> and select the <u>type of account</u> you want your S&P500 fund in. I discuss investment custodians and account types below.

<u>Types of investment custodians:</u> The custodian is who you send your investment dollars to. You trust them to invest your money, return it to you when you ask, and not spend it on a vacation to Tahiti. There are two types of custodians for you to contribute your money to: brokers and mutual funds. Brokers will accept your investment checks and then purchase and sell investments on your behalf according to your direction. They charge a fee for this service. The investments may also charge additional investment related expense. Examples of brokers are TD Ameritrade, Ameriprise, Merrill Lynch, and many others. The people who call you or email you telling you about great investments are all brokers.

Mutual funds accept your investment checks and then invest money on your behalf. Each mutual fund has certain high level guidelines (e.g. S&P 500 index, Large Cap, or International Value). They buy and sell investments on their own within the guidelines according to their best judgment. You split the brokerage fees and investment expenses with the thousands or millions of other people who are investing their money in the same mutual fund. Your share of expenses is usually much less than if you used a brokerage account. Examples of good mutual fund families are Vanguard, Fidelity, Schwab, Janus, although most of these firms also offer brokerage services for their clients as an add-on.

I prefer mutual funds.

There are also several types of accounts to consider. Each account type has different rules regarding taxes and investment options. The main account types to consider are: 401(k), IRA, and taxable account. Investment custodians will generally set up whichever account type you ask.

401(k) -- These accounts are through your employer. They have the advantage of allowing contributions directly from your paycheck. Another advantage is that many employers will also contribute to your account. They also have the advantage of being "pre-tax" up to $18,000 for most people. A pre-tax contribution means that money you earn and contribute directly to a 401(k) doesn't count as income at tax time. Disadvantages are that withdrawals count as income, and an extra 10% tax is levied on withdrawals made before retirement, and investment expenses are a little bit higher. When you leave your job, you can rollover all the money from your 401(k) to your IRA. I generally recommend this because IRAs have slightly lower investment expenses.

IRA -- You set up an IRA on your own, independent from your employer. Allowable contributions are much lower-- only $5,500 for most people. Investment expenses are lower than for IRAs for 401(k)s. You can set up this account to be "pre-tax" (Traditional) or "after - tax" (Roth). Generally, if you believe your tax rate in retirement will be higher than it is now, you should choose a Roth IRA, because retirement withdrawals are tax free for Roth IRAs. If you believe your tax rate will go down in retirement, then you should stick with a Traditional IRA.

Taxable Account -- There are no limits to your contributions to a taxable account. However whenever you receive investment income or sell one of your investments at a profit you will have to pay taxes on the investment gains. The biggest advantage to a taxable account is that you may make withdrawals whenever you want without penalty. A taxable investment account is best if you have already contributed a significant amount to the retirement accounts and you still have additional money available for investing but you want to leave your options open to use it before retirement. Most people should consider a taxable account only after they have contributed as much as they legally can to their 401(k) / IRA retirement accounts. Investment dollars are for the long term, so the advantage of being able to withdraw from your taxable account is small compared to the cost of paying taxes on all of your investment gains between now and the end of time.

Chapter 5 - Roth or not Roth

Your first investment accounts will more likely than not be either a 401(k) and / or an IRA. There are a few life events that often come up related to these accounts. It is worth it to go through these events and understand how they may affect your retirement accounts.

You need some money for a large one time purchase (e.g. car, down payment on a house). You are informed that your 401(k) will permit you to borrow money from the 401(k) account at a better interest rate than you can get elsewhere. As a bonus, all the interest you pay on the loan is added to your 401(k) balance. Should you borrow the money?

It's not a slam dunk, but it might be a good option. Before you say yes, consider these downsides:

Whenever you leave your employer, for any reason, whether you quit or were fired, you have 60 days to pay back the balance in full. So if you take out a $20K loan to buy a car and are fired in six months with a $17K outstanding balance on the loan, you've got 60 days after you lost your paycheck to come up with $17K. If you don't, the $17K is considered a 401(k) withdrawal. As a result it is taxable income and subject to a 10% penalty because it is an ineligible withdrawal from your retirement account. For most middle class people that will amount to a 25% to 35% tax bill on the loan or ($4250 to $5950). That's a big chunk of change for somebody who is unemployed. Before taking out the loan, you need a concrete plan on how to pay it back in the event you lose your job.

Another downside to a 401(k) loan is that your paycheck goes down because the 401(k) plan takes your loan payment directly from your paycheck. You get what's left. If you can't take a cut in your net pay, you shouldn't be getting this loan.

A third downside is that your money is no longer invested if you take a 401(k) loan. Your 401(k) withdrawal is taken out of the mutual funds in your 401(k) account, thereby reducing your investment gains. The investment gains lost due to the 401(k) loan are slightly offset by the interest payments back into your 401(k) account. Over the long term, though, the interest payments will be considerably less than the return on your account if your money had stayed invested.

You are leaving your job. What do you do with your 401(k)?

Remember, your 401(k) account is yours and the contributions and earnings on the contributions that you made are also yours. Your former employer has no access to it.

Some 401(k) plans allow you to do nothing. Your money stays invested and investment gains continue to be applied to your account. You can no longer contribute to or borrow from these accounts, though.

Doing nothing is certainly the easiest option, and sometimes it is even a decent option to choose.

You may be eligible to contribute to a different 401(k)- either from a second job you currently have or from your new job. If so you can execute a rollover to your new company 401(k). You should consider this if your new employer has better, lower cost investment options.

If you do this, make sure your rollover is sent by the 401(k) custodian of your former employer directly to the 401(k) custodian of your new employer. If the 401(k) ends up in your possession for more than 60 days, it's no longer a rollover. Guess what? It's now your withdrawal. You lost your right to put it in another retirement account. You're also getting a 1099 form counting that as income. And, you're paying a 10% penalty on top of that. Big mistake, don't do that.

Finally, you are always eligible to rollover your 401(k) into an IRA. This is usually the most advantageous option even though it requires a bit more paperwork (fifteen minutes to an hour). The reason why this option is usually best is because IRAs have lower administrative expenses than 401(k)s, and low cost IRA providers pass on that expense savings to you. For example, Vanguard IRAs have an expense ratio about 0.2% lower for their IRAs than for their 401(k)s. That's about $100 per year for a $50K retirement account. Sure that expense isn't going to make or break you, but why take on the expense if you don't have to?

Rolling over a 401(k) into an IRA requires you to open an IRA and fill out the paperwork to rollover the money from your 401(k). If you already have an IRA you can rollover your 401(k) money directly to your existing IRA.

My employer is having financial difficulties. Should I take my money out of the 401(k) plan for safekeeping?

No way. There's no reason to. 401(k) plans are set up so that your employer has no access to the accounts. The custodian of the 401(k) plan (e.g. Schwab) is holding and controlling all of the assets. Even if your employer goes bankrupt your 401(k) money will be safe with the 401(k) custodian. You definitely don't want to take on the taxes and penalties with this move.

However if your employer goes bankrupt, you'll likely be unemployed. In this case you may want to explore rolling your 401(k) money to an IRA after you lose your job.

Chapter 6 - IRA issues

This chapter is for issues and opportunities you may encounter after you have been investing for a few years. It's good to know the rules, regulations, benefits, and consequences of these investing actions.

Roth IRA - Investing in a Roth IRA is almost exactly the same as investing in a Traditional IRA. You fill out the paperwork with the same custodian in exactly the same way (except you check "Roth" instead of "Traditional" under "IRA Type"); you have the same investment choices; and you get the same benefit of not paying taxes on the investment gains within the Roth IRA account. There are two main differences between a Roth and a Traditional IRA:

1. Contributions to Traditional IRAs are tax deductible; contributions to Roth IRAs are not. If you are in the 25% tax bracket, your $5000 Traditional IRA contribution will reduce your taxes this year by $1250 ($5000 x 25% = $1250).

2. Withdrawals from Traditional IRAs are taxable; withdrawals from Roth IRAs are not. If you are in the 15% tax bracket when you retire, your $5000 Traditional IRA withdrawal will reduce your taxes by $750 ($5000 x 15% = $750).

So, you do pay taxes on IRA contributions no matter what. With Roth IRAs you pay taxes now, with Traditional IRAs you pay taxes later. A great way to game the difference between the two IRAs is to contribute to a Traditional IRA when your income tax bracket is higher than usual. When this occurs your deduction will reduce your taxes more.

You should always contribute to a Roth IRA when your income tax bracket is lower than usual, the loss of the tax deduction won't cost you very much now; however the benefit of having tax free income when you are over 60 and are in a higher tax bracket will be much larger.

Several years ago I very successfully played that game. The first year I was ramping up my consulting business I made almost no money after business expenses. I was in the 0% tax bracket! That means I made less than $10,000 after deductions. What a great time to contribute to a Roth. I took money from my savings and wrote a check into my Roth account. I didn't get a deduction, but I didn't care. My income was too low to be paying any taxes anyway. That money is going to be invested in the Roth account for a few decades before I take it out. When I do take my money out of the Roth account, the account will probably be a lot larger and I still won't pay any taxes. No taxes in, no taxes on the decades of investment gains, and no taxes out. What a great deal for me.

How was I able to afford a Roth contribution in a year where I made less than $10,000 you ask? From savings, of course. Remember, a Roth contribution is not an expense, it is a smart way to allocate your savings.

Traditional to Roth IRA Rollover - Performing this move is just like a turbocharged version of choosing the Roth IRA in the first place. You can, at any time you wish, fill out some paperwork with your Traditional IRA custodian, and the assets in your Traditional IRA will be transferred to a Roth IRA. This new Roth IRA will look and act exactly the same as the Traditional IRA until you retire and start to withdraw money. Your Roth IRA withdrawals will be tax free. The catch is that your rollover counts as income this year and will increase your tax bill this year. So the strategy with a rollover is to perform the rollover in a year where you have a lower than typical income. Then make sure you don't roll over so much that you are pushed into a higher income tax bracket.

Let's take an example: A married couple who usually has a combined income of $100K is in the 25% tax bracket (the 25% tax bracket starts at a net income of about $70K). One year they have a poor earnings year and earns only $30K due to unemployment. This married couple is likely to have $15K to $20K of deductions, so the couple's taxable income is only $15K. This puts the couple barely in the 15% income tax bracket.

This is a great year to rollover some funds from a Traditional IRA to a Roth. I'd recommend the couple rollover up to $55K to a Roth IRA. A $55K rollover will increase their net income to $70K ($15K earned income + $55K rollover = $70K). They would still be in the 15% tax bracket even after the rollover. The $55K rollover will increase their tax bill when they complete their tax return next year by $8250 ($8250 = $55K rollover x 15% tax bracket). They should pay this tax bill out of their savings.

Now remember the $55K roll over will double possibly three times (assuming the couple is reasonably young) and grow to $440K ($55K x 2 x 2 x 2 = $440K). Then when the couple retires and chooses to withdraw the money from their IRA they would have to pay taxes on the entire $440K withdrawal without the rollover.

A 35% tax rate in retirement is entirely plausible under current tax law for strong savers. Often savers are in a higher tax bracket when they retire because their social security income, pension income (maybe), and IRA income combines to a higher income than their salaried income from when they were working.

Finally, if the couple doesn't do the rollover and then decides to withdraw the entire $440K at once for a major purchase after retirement, they would be in one of the highest tax brackets. The $440K withdrawal in retirement might be taxed at a 35% tax rate or more. If the $440K retirement withdrawal is taxed at 35%, that tax bill will come to $154K! I'd gladly pay $8250 in tax on a rollover today in order to save a $154K tax bill down the line. And you should too. Your future self will thank you.

Borrow from Your Retirement Plan- It sounds like a can't miss proposition. You need some money fast. You can fill out some paperwork and turn some of the value of your retirement plan into cash in your checking account to pay for that surprisingly expensive trip you took to Vegas last month. No credit check required. All the interest payments to your loan are returned to you in the form of additional retirement plan contributions. How nice! What could go wrong?

Borrowing from your retirement plan is kind of like borrowing from the mafia. It is really nice in the beginning and is a great idea as long as you play according to the rules. But if you break the rules, even by a little bit, things will go terribly wrong and you'll wish you never took out the loan at all.

Here's how borrowing from your retirement plan works. After you fill out the paperwork, you get a check and your 401(k) arranges for a paycheck deduction of your loan payments plus interest. These payments are deposited back in your 401(k).

If you quit or get fired before the 401(k) loan is paid off, you get a bill for the outstanding balance. If you don't pay the bill in 60 days, the outstanding balance is converted to an unauthorized early withdrawal. The tax bill on these are huge.

First, the withdrawal is considered income, and you will have to pay income tax on that withdrawal. Most middle class people are in the 15%, 25%, or 28% income tax bracket. Next, there is a tax penalty of

10%, so add that amount to your income tax bracket. For example, if you have a $5000 outstanding 401(k) loan balance that you don't pay back within 30 days after leaving your job, your tax bill could be 38% of the balance (28% tax bracket plus 10% penalty). At tax time you'll be paying $1,900 extra in taxes ($5,000 x 38% = $1,900). That's an incredible net worth killer. Instead of having $5,000 in your 401(k), you have a tax bill of $1,900. And, need I remind you, all of this happens on top of your job loss. That's a pretty significant financial disaster. That's why I generally don't recommend that you borrow from your retirement plan.

Even if you have no risk of job loss, there's another important concern to borrowing from your retirement plan.

If you borrow from your retirement plan, your net pay will go down. So, if you had trouble making ends meet before, you are really going to have trouble now. This can lead to a terrible downward financial spiral.

You borrow from your 401(k), your net pay goes down and then use your savings to make up the shortfall. Eventually your savings runs out and an unexpected expense comes along. So you may start racking up the balance on your credit card. Now you have a lower net pay and a new expense - 29% credit card interest. Before you know it you've set yourself all the way back to step one of getting control of your financial life.

So yes you can borrow from your retirement plan, and it can work out well. However, when it doesn't work out well, it can be a complete disaster to your finances. I don't think it is worth the risk and I recommend against it.

Margin Account - This option is available to you if you have saved your way up to having a taxable investment account. Borrowing on margin can be a good idea in the right circumstances. It essentially is a loan you get from your taxable brokerage account. There are no costs to set up the loan. There's no credit checks or income verification. There's no set repayment schedule. These are all great loan features.

When you borrow on margin, you complete paperwork that agrees to the following:

- You aren't going to borrow more than 50% of the value of the stocks in your brokerage account on the date of your loan.
- The broker adds interest onto the outstanding balance of the loan.
- The proceeds from all dividends, stock sales, and new contributions are automatically used to pay down the loan.
- Under no circumstances can the outstanding balance of your loan ever exceed 70% of the value of the stocks in your account (this can happen if the value of your stock portfolio declines significantly).

- If the value of your stock portfolio does drop so far as to make the balance of your loan more than 70% of the value of your stock portfolio, **your broker can sell any or all of the stocks in your portfolio at current market prices. This is called a "margin call".** Your broker will then use the proceeds of the sale to pay off part of the loan until the balance of the loan falls below 70%. That is called a "margin call". You don't get any cash, but you do now have a smaller stock portfolio.

So borrowing on margin is usually a great deal. However, when things go wrong, they go really wrong. Here's an example of how things can go wrong. Let's say you have a $100K brokerage account that is set up to allow you to borrow on margin. Most of your account is invested in stock shares for your employer because you believe in the company and the new product it is developing. You decide to borrow $50K on margin from this account for a down payment on a house. You still have $100K invested in company stock.

Over the next six months, a recession hits your industry. The value of your company stock declines to $85K; Your margin loan is at $51K ($1K in interest was added on to the loan). The outstanding balance of your loan is now at 60%. Over the next three months a series of bad (unfairly in your opinion) industry reports come out about reduced expectations for the success of your company's upcoming product launch. The value of your stock drops by almost 50% to $50K. You are continuously getting hit with margin calls. Your brokerage firm over that time sells all of your company stock. The $50K or so of proceeds from the stock sale all went to pay off the mortgage loan. Your brokerage account is depleted. Six months after this fiasco you were proven right. The industry reports were wrong. The product launch indeed was a great success. If you had held on to the original $100K worth of shares, you would have a $200K portfolio now. Instead you have nothing. All because of that terribly timed margin call.

I don't want to discourage you about margin loans. They can work great. And I have successfully borrowed on margin in the past. Here are a few guidelines to protect you from the worst case picture painted above:

- Although you are allowed to borrow 50% of your portfolio, limit yourself to 30% as an added layer of protection. If you only borrow 30%, your portfolio would have to decline in value by 57% before you could be threatened with a margin call. These situations are rare, and usually take some time to develop, allowing you room to develop a plan to pay back the margin loan before the margin call occurs.
- Only borrow on margin against a diversified portfolio. If you just have one or two stocks, the potential for large market moves is much

higher. Diversified portfolios move in a much more narrow range making margin calls much less likely.

I have followed the two rules above and never had a margin call.

Fund your own business with your IRA - There are many types of investments permitted by IRAs. In addition to stocks and bonds, IRAs can also invest in private businesses. Why not use your IRA money to invest in a business you own? Of course you would be president of that business and be paid handsomely.

Every franchise expo / small business seminar has someone pitching this idea. Business brokers often suggest this approach to financing a business purchase. There's some really significant risks to this approach. Foremost, it may not even be legal.

IRS rules list as a prohibited transaction any transaction that allows you to handle the money or personally benefit from investments in your IRA. It's going to be hard to argue with the IRS that if you are the handsomely paid president of a company owned by your IRA and you are not personally benefitting from your IRA investment.

Your entire IRA is disqualified if you personally benefit. That means the <u>entire</u> IRA is considered to be distributed to you on the day the IRS disqualifies it. The entire balance is considered taxable income. The

IRS also slaps a 10% early distribution penalty on top of the taxes if you are under 59 1/2. It's not worth the risk. Don't use your IRA to start your new business no matter what the huckster at the small business expo is telling you. He's not going to pay the price if things go bad, you are.

Even if you could be sure it was legal, it still is probably not a good idea. The worst case scenario can really send you into financial ruin. If your startup business goes bad, and statistics say that is very likely, you will be unemployed, and your life's retirement savings will have collapsed to $0. That's a very deep hole to dig out of before retirement. If this happens, it is likely that your retirement will end up being a significantly lower lifestyle than what you would otherwise receive.

Chapter 7 - Time to Sell the House

So, you've lived in your house five, six, seven years or so. You've received a few pay bumps during that time. You can easily afford a higher mortgage payment. It's time to sell the house and move up to a bigger, better house. Or is it?

Virtually everyone in the real estate industry - banks, mortgage brokers, realtors, and your mother in law will ask you "How much house can you afford". If you don't know how much you can afford, they'll be more than happy to figure it out for you. Once you know how much you can afford, they will suggest that number should be the budget for your next home purchase. What a ridiculous approach to making a purchase decision.

Imagine going to the grocery store to buy milk and hearing the store manager say "how much milk can you afford"?

You look over to him and say "I don't know. I have $100 in my wallet".

He smiles at you and says "Today milk costs $4 a gallon, you can afford 25 gallons of milk. Pop open your trunk and I'll help you load it in."

You'd never go for that at the grocery store and you definitely shouldn't go for that same approach when used by the real estate industry.

You should only trade up if you are really dissatisfied with some aspect of your house, and spending more money will deliver you a house that will make you happy.

So, maybe you are unhappy with your house. Maybe you got a new job and want to move closer to your new office. Maybe the size of your family is changing and you now need a differently sized house. There are plenty of good reasons to buy a new house. But "because I can afford it" isn't one of them.

Most people selling their house are also buying a new one at the same time. Navigating two of the biggest financial transactions of your life virtuously simultaneously can cause stress for anyone. At times it can be very difficult to make the timing work correctly since you don't have full control of when the closing happens for either your purchase or your sale. If the timing is bad, one of two things can happen:

1. You sell your current house before you buy your new house. You become homeless (for a short time).

2. You reach the closing of your new house purchase and haven't sold your current house yet. You don't have the money to pay for the new house because you were counting on cash from the old house.

Neither of these scenarios are the end of the world, so you can take a deep breath and relax. If #1 happens, you can put your stuff in storage, then you can live in a hotel, take a vacation, or rent an apartment. If #2 happens, you can ask for an extension or move on to a different house. However, all things being equal, I'd rather be in situation #1 than #2. Situation #2 puts your initial deposit on the new home in jeopardy. The people selling you your new home can say "tough doody," to your request and keep your deposit if you don't close the deal as you promised.

So, when buying a new house, I recommend you close on selling your old home first, before putting a deposit on a new home. People can sense desperation, and some homebuyers may seek to take advantage of your desperation. It can go something like this.

You and the buyers of your old home are sitting at the closing table. The buyer says "I was looking at the inspection report again, and I didn't realize the extent of the costs related to the repairs needed for your house. There's $5000 more in repairs than you initially led me to believe. You need to give me $5000 for these repairs, otherwise I can't go through with the purchase." You can apply the "tough doody" approach and keep their deposit, but the person buying your home might call your bluff believing you want to move on with your life and not lose the deposit on your purchase more than you want that $5000. And let's face it, the buyer is probably right. You'll cave in and give him the $5000. As you are writing the check, you'll be thinking "If I hadn't put the deposit down on my new house, I'd never agree to giving this jerk $5000".

So don't get yourself in that bind, make sure to delay your purchase until you've sold your old place. A short term rental is much cheaper than $5000 extorted from you at the closing table.

Step 1 in selling your place is to find a good real estate broker. Yes, they charge a lot of money, often in the neighborhood of $15,000 for a mid level house. They make a few phone calls, show the house a few times, and get their commission check, apparently getting you to pay them over $1000 per hour for their time.

Don't worry about the broker's finances. Focus on your own. A good broker might be able to sell your house six months earlier than you otherwise could; a good broker can also, through negotiating on your behalf convince a buyer to pay $10K or $20K more than they otherwise would. I will gladly pay someone $15K to make $20K more on my house. I don't care how much he makes per hour.

I actually witnessed the value of a good broker firsthand when I bought an investment property a few years ago. I was looking for an investment property for a few months mainly by driving around neighborhoods that I wanted to invest in and contacting owners with "for sale" signs". I hadn't found anything that I thought was a good deal. A broker who I had never met before sent an email about a property that looked like a good deal. I scheduled an appointment and got to see the place. I liked it and made an offer.

During the negotiation I made an offer that I believed the seller would agree to. The seller was desperate to sell because he was facing foreclosure. I was confident that he would move by $15K or so in order to avoid foreclosure. When things stalled, the broker stepped in and reminded me that the sale was a very good deal and that if I decided to walk away he might choose to buy the property himself. "What a line of BS," I said to myself as we ended our conversation. Over the next day I acknowledged "well, there's a small chance the broker wasn't talking BS and I don't want to lose this great deal over a few thousand dollars." I upped my offer and we closed the deal. The broker earned the money the seller paid him by finding me, and then convincing me to pay just a little bit more.

Once you have your broker. Invite him over and listen to him. He may tell you to paint the house, or make some repairs. He probably will have ideas on the appropriate asking price. **Take his suggestions. He is as motivated as you are to sell your house and he has much more experience than you in selling houses.**

Chapter 8 - Writing a Will

If you answer yes to both of these questions then you need a will: 1) Will you die someday? 2) Do you have any possessions at all?

If you've read this far, it means you need a will. Most wills are pretty similar. For married people the most common will is "All to spouse. If we both die, all divided equally among the kids. Aunt Betty will be the kids' guardian." When you go to an estate planning attorney (a lawyer who deals with wills) to draft a will, she'll charge you $1000 or so and turn those simple last wishes into a 25 page document.

Before you hire an estate planning attorney to write your will, I suggest you and your spouse thoroughly think through what else you want your will to say. Actually write it out in plain English, at least in outline form. Your estate planning attorney will incorporate your outline into a legal will. Beyond the standard will spelled out in the above paragraph, consider the following:

Nobody can inherit assets they don't know about. As part of your will and probably attached to your will should be a listing of all of your assets, account numbers, approximate value and contact information of the entity that can turn your assets into cash for your heirs. This document should list bank accounts, retirement accounts, life insurance policies, annuities, work death benefits, debts owed to you, your social security information (Social Security pays out death benefits in some cases), and valuable non-financial assets (e.g. car, stamp collection).

You need a backup heir in case your kids also die. Sure it's very unlikely, but family tragedies do happen. Decide what you want to have happen to your assets if it does happen. If you don't write down your wishes, your assets will go to your closest blood relatives, whether you like them or not. This family tragedy section of the will could also get activated if your named heirs pass away before you die and you forget to update your will.

Explain your wishes. Of course you don't have to explain what you are doing with your money. You can do whatever you want with your money. But you don't want to risk having your heirs, or the people who thought they would be your heirs misinterpret the rationale behind the instructions contained in your will. As an example, my grandfather had thirteen children. When he died, his children learned that the will provided a different amount of money for each of them. Nobody except grandpa knows why. And he's not talking.

Nothing in your will should be a surprise. This advice is controversial in some circles. Some people believe that a will is a secret document and the contents shouldn't be shared until you are gone. I completely disagree. Shortly after a loved one passes away is no time for surprises. Your heirs and those that are close to you should know if they are in or out of the will, what they are inheriting and the approximate value far in advance of your death.

Some may feel this advice is controversial. Some people feel if their heirs know how much money they will be inheriting, the heirs will become lazy, or even worse, they would be wishing for your life to end. This isn't very well thought out reasoning. An inheritance that is known about years, or even decades in advance can be planned for both emotionally and financially. Knowing about an inheritance allows a person to incorporate that information into their own financial life. Once the inheritance takes place at an unknown date in the future, there will be no sudden shocks to the heirs' lifestyle. As for the second concern-- that your heirs will wish for your death once they find out how much money they are getting-- well, if you really feel that way you might want to consider selecting different heirs. I don't want anyone who prefers my money over my life to get any of my money at all.

Choose an executor. Now choose a backup executor. The executor of a will is an adult that is capable of carrying out the instructions contained in the will. The most common executor is the primary heir. Another common selection is a close family friend who is respected by your heirs as able to make intelligent and fair decisions regarding the division of assets among multiple heirs. A third common choice is the attorney drafting your will. Whoever you choose, you need to ask them if she will accept that responsibility and workload. If she says "no," or is hesitant, select someone else. Also it is best you don't select someone much older than you to be the executor of your estate. You want to be sure that she will be around after you are gone.

Once you've chosen your executor and she has accepted, tell your heirs as well as anybody that might have the expectation that she will be named as the executor. Explain your choice. Of course you don't have to, but it is worthwhile to do so to prevent hurt feelings. Some people feel that it is a special honor to be selected as an executor. However, the appropriate selection is more dependent on who is best suited for the task rather than who holds the most honored position in your heart. Good qualities for an executor include:

- Skills at managing money decisions
- Respect from your heirs
- Integrity
- The available time to handle your affairs
- Understanding of your financial situation and wishes
- Living nearby
- Good health and future life expectancy.

The duties of an executor can often involve significant time and stress. I believe it is reasonable and fair to compensate your executor for fulfilling their duties. You can construct this compensation as a fee or an inheritance. If the executor is getting a fee, then they will have to pay income tax on the fee they receive once they complete their duties. If the executor is getting an inheritance, it will be tax-free. However, the inheritance will be delivered even if your chosen executor doesn't fulfill her duties. Either arrangement can be appropriate. it's your call.

Sit down with your executor. Once you and your spouse have decided on the executor of your will. Invite the executor over and explain the intentions of your will. Describe an overview of your financial situation and discuss what you would like to happen and listen to your executor's thoughts as well. This conversation should be designed to give your executor the information to be able to do a good job. It will also give both you and your executor confidence that she is up to the job.

Decide if your kids should inherit all the money right away. If you have the standard "all to spouse, then to kids" will, your kids can potentially get a big pile of cash for their 18th birthday. And if that happens, they will have the big pile of cash without you to guide them on the best way to manage such a windfall. "but I'm not rich," you say. Think harder. Do you have a house with equity? That equity will turn into cash. Do you have a life insurance policy, either that you purchase, or one that is purchased by your employer? That will turn into cash too. Do you have a college fund for your kids? When your kids are 18, it's their money, they may not choose to use it for college anymore. Retirement assets... The list goes on.

Not to mention, if your untimely death occurs due to an accident that is somebody else's fault, there is a decent chance that the at fault party in the accident will be delivering a six or seven figure payout to your kids.

Now think about whether you think your kids will be ready-- intellectually or emotionally-- to handle that kind of money when they turn 18. Will they blow it? Will the money cause them to make dumb decisions in their lives, will the money make them lazy? You remember when you were 18. If you had $100 in your pocket, that was more than enough money to have a great time. More than that might be more of a curse than a blessing.

If you wish, you can create a provision in your will that money will be left in trust for your kids until they reach a certain age, say 25 years old. That means the money gets invested, and nobody can withdraw the funds. You can even create a provision where money is held in trust until different life milestones occur, for example, college graduation, marriage, buying a home. I don't favor these milestone provisions. Your offspring should live the lives they choose, not the life you choose. I do favor the age provision, though. The provision in my will says my son inherits money in equal proportions when he is 25, 30, and 35. That means he can screw up money management twice and still be left with something. He's going to read this book, though, so I expect him to get it right the first time.

Choose a financial representative for your kids.
You need a provision like this if there is any chance of your passing away before you want your kids to be managing their inheritance (Read: if your kids can't handle their whole inheritance right now, then they need a financial representative). A selection of a financial representative is often overlooked because many assume that your kids' guardian will also manage the inheritance. However, it is often true that the person you believe is best able to take care of your kids is different from the person you believe is best able to take care of your kids inheritance. In addition, it might not be the best idea in the world to give Aunt Betty unlimited access to your kids inheritance. Sure, your trust Aunt Betty with all your heart but... one day Aunt Betty's Visa bill may be a bit too high... she may recall she's taken the kids out for ice cream an awful lot this month causing the Visa bill to be so high...she may feel $2500 from the trust fund should cover all the expenses.

In short your kids need a financial representative. This person should be a trustworthy friend of yours with similar financial values. This representative will have the authority to send money from the trust fund to Aunt Betty to spend on your kids whenever there is a justifiable expense. You may want to specify a monthly allowance as well. This would be the best way to preserve your kids inheritance while still providing for their childhood.

Keep a copy of your will on your computer and revisit every few years. Lastly, once you get your will written, don't just throw it in a safety deposit box and forget about it. Keep a copy on your computer as well. Set an appointment with your spouse to review the will every three years or so. See if you need to change anything. Maybe Aunt Betty joins a cult and is no longer a suitable guardian for your kids, maybe you become considerably more wealthy and want to spread your wealth around further than just your kids. Maybe lots of things. A will is definitely something that always needs to be kept up to date because you never know when you're going to need yours.

Chapter 9 - Talking Money with Your Adult Kids

To many, talking about money with their kids is like talking about sex. It's dirty. It's something that people just shouldn't do. I disagree! The more you share your financial life with your kids, the more they will be able to benefit from the financial education you have developed over the years through the school of hard knocks. Personal finance is learned best by experience and example, rather than by textbook education (notice how this book has lots of examples, and very few textbook definitions of personal finance terms).

I recommend that you make your financial life an open book with your teenage and adult kids. For one thing, your kids want to have an understanding on how strong your finances are. They want to know if they should plan to help with your expenses as you age, or not.

Your kids also deserve to learn about the smart and not so smart financial moves that you have made in your life. If they learn these moves, they can copy your smart moves, and avoid your mistakes.

Last, if you are open with your kids about your finances, you may find them becoming more open with you about their finances. This will open the door to allowing you to advise them through financial situations you have gone through that they may be currently experiencing.

Lastly, since you can't take it with you, your kids will likely inherit your financial situation as well as your assets. It would be very helpful to them if they know how you arrived at the financial situation you are in. They should understand why you are invested in the investments you have. Then they can better determine what to do with those investments after you are gone.

When I was a teenager and young adult I knew everything about my mother's finances. It was part of our family's culture. I knew how much money she earned, I knew about all her bills and expenses. I knew about her mortgage balance, and the mortgage terms. I even knew where her bank accounts were, the insurance policies she had, and why. Little did either of us know, that my mother would become terminally ill when I was only 24 years old. She had the confidence in my knowledge of her finances to provide me with a power of attorney over her financial affairs as she got sicker. I had the confidence and ability to take over her finances at that time without having to pester her with dozens of financial questions. Her openness with her financial situation over the years was all the pre-work she needed to do to reduce the stress of moving her financial responsibilities to me. And that was definitely a time in both of our lives when we needed to reduce our stress in every way possible.

If you don't currently have an open relationship with your kids with regard to personal finance, I recommend you introduce the topic as you would tell your life story. Except with this story, focus all of your energy on telling the story of your income and expenses, assets and debts. As you bring the story into present day, include an increasing amount of detail-- include what you did, and why. Include who you have financial relationships and why. Explain why you ended any financial relationships you've had in the recent past as well.

Chapter 10 - Talking Money with Your Parents

My initial temptation with this chapter is to just copy the "Talking Money with Your Adult Kids" chapter, except reverse where it says kids to where it says parents. But then I decided to get serious. This discussion can be much more challenging, but can also be much more important.

If you are part of a family that does not have an open relationship with money, any discussion about money may be very tough and meet heavy resistance. After all, parents who are not open about money have decades of experience reinforcing that behavior. They also likely had role models in their early life that taught them to be secretive about money. One initial query will not be enough to undo this conditioning.

In addition to the conditioning not to talk about money with anyone, your parents especially don't want to talk about money with you. They are used to telling you what to do. They remember when you bet your entire life savings of $25 on the Super Bowl and lost. Any discussion you initiate about money with them may imply to them that you think you can educate them about money; and that thought is ridiculous to them because they remember the Super Bowl bet.

So, you may have to ease into this discussion over a period of time. There are a few good openers to this topic.

- Sharing your own financial life and asking your parents how they would handle your situation.
- Getting an understanding of your parents' values around money.
- Discussing personal finance issues in the news.
- Sharing how your get your personal finance advice / information.
- Maybe even a copy of this book!

This isn't a psychology book, so I can't lay out the complete roadmap and minefields on how to get your parents to be more open with you about money. However, you do need to get them there. It's important. Keep trying until you succeed, even if it takes you years.

Once you get the communication flowing, here's what you need to discuss.

Their finances and yours. Do they have enough cash flow? Are they, or will they need financial help in order to live a lifestyle that you both are comfortable with. If you are going to be helping out your parents one day, it's better to know now. If you have that discussion now, you can prepare for that financial expense, and they can have the comfort of knowing they will be able to maintain their current lifestyle.

On the other hand, if their financial situation is stronger than yours, knowledge of their ability and willingness (or inability and unwillingness) to help you out in your expenses can help you manage your finances effectively for the future.

Do they have a will? Make sure the answer is "yes". If not, help them get in touch with an estate attorney that can prepare a will for them. Then find out if you have any responsibilities in the will. You need to know and prepare if you are the executor (see the chapter on wills for more on this). If you are not the executor, make sure your parents inform their executor of the responsibilities.

Get an understanding of how they are managing their finances. I think this is one of the toughest parts of the conversation about money. Some parents view this part of the conversation as an intrusion into their personal affairs. Some view it as an insult and a demonstration that they are perceived as not being up to the task of managing money.

It doesn't have to be that way. The conversation can start by mentioning that you need an understanding of their entire money situation so that you can manage the portfolio intelligently in the event you are called upon to do so. This approach to the conversation puts both of you on the same page with the same goals-- ensuring your parents hard earned wealth is managed intelligently no matter what.

Have they documented their entire net worth picture. Assets have no value to heirs if the heirs don't know about them or don't have enough information to access those assets. Your parents should remember to include life insurance, long - term care insurance, and any annuity or workplace insurance policies that provide for death benefits. In their documentation they should include the following information: investment type / Investment institution / account number / approximate value / and contact information of the institution. In my life I was very fortunate that my mother did this before she died. It was all on one sheet of paper in her safety deposit box. In just one day I was able to set the wheels in motion to have her assets transferred over. By reading that information sheet I even learned that there was a small life insurance policy that her employer paid for. I was able to collect the proceeds on this policy. Without my mom's information sheet I never would have known about that policy and never would have received the life insurance benefit.

Who are they getting advice from. You may need to contact your parents' advisers some day. It's good to know who these people are. Some people have multiple advisers for different aspects of their investment life. Be sure to find contact information for the attorney that holds their will, their financial adviser(s) (if any), their CPA, and any other person that has access to their investments or the ability to influence their investment decisions.

There's a special case for this item. Some people aren't getting any financial advice from anyone. They are managing their finances and investment portfolio 100% based on their own financial expertise. This isn't necessarily bad. How can I say that? I am one of those people. While I did hire an estate attorney to prepare my will, I do not have any financial advisers or tax preparers. I do that myself, that's my thing.

For people with parents in that boat, your job is to understand how they are making financial decisions. Once you understand how, you can make sure your parents have the knowledge and intellectual capacity to make intelligent financial decisions. In this case, it is also important to take action if you observe any cognitive decline in your parents.

Chapter 11 - A Whole Chapter on Life insurance and Annuities

How much life insurance is too much life insurance? I don't know, but it's less than your financial advisor Recommends

The correct answer to how much life insurance to buy is "It depends…" There is no great "rule of thumb", If anyone answers any differently, they are either ignorant of the purpose of life insurance, trying to sell you something (life insurance), or both.

When my wife and I first got married, we went to a "financial advisor" who worked at a large, well-known financial advisory firm. After we completed an initial questionnaire stating our income, assets, and liabilities, the advisor came back to us with a three ring binder full of recommendations (to buy their products). One of the recommendations was for my wife to buy a $3 million policy on me (about 20 years income). As background, I was 38 and my wife was pregnant with our first child. We were both employed in professional jobs.

Here's how my conversation with the financial advisor went –

> Financial advisor: We recommend you purchase a whole life policy of $3 million. This is what we calculate is needed to continue to support your wife in the lifestyle you both are accustomed to."

Me: "That sounds like a lot. Are you saying that my wife will end up destitute if somebody doesn't hand her a check for $3 million on the day that I die?

FA: Well, our formulas state that is how much is needed to replace your expected future income.

Me: So what?

We didn't buy any life insurance (or any other financial products) from the advisor. Now maybe saying 'so what?' is rude; but trying to guilt me into spending thousands of dollars on a product I don't need is even more rude.

Now back to the 'so what?'. The "advisor" used the "income replacement method" to determine our financial need. Interestingly, when I was taking Certified Financial Planner coursework, we learned five methods for calculating life insurance need. The income replacement method usually resulted in the highest life insurance need. My instructor, who sold life insurance in addition to being a CFP, told us that this method was "the best". I learned this method because the instructor grades my exam. Later in the course one of the students who happened to also work for him stated "I have never met anyone that didn't need more life insurance." That student definitely passed the class and is now a financial adviser.

Coincidentally, The adviser my wife and I visited used the "how can I get the biggest commission method" to determine that I needed a whole life policy. The income replacement method is a calculation to determine how much money is needed to be put in a conservative investment account today to allow the account to pay all of the future paychecks I am expected to earn for the rest of my life. It's an interesting calculation, but so what?

The income replacement method gets the maximum amount of life insurance a person could possibly need. For 99.9% of families the life insurance need is much less. You would only need the income replacement amount of life insurance if several very unlikely conditions are all met:

- Your family's expenses do not go down after you die. (Unless you are a monk who lives in a cave, expenses will go down because all of your personal expenses will disappear).
- Your family spends 100% of your income on themselves. (i.e. a real "keep up with the Joneses" family that spends every dollar before it burns a hole in their pocket).
- Your family has no alternate source of income. (any spouse is going to get a job at some point, maybe not until the kids move out, but at some point…).
- Your family has no savings. (hopefully that is not true).

Unfortunately many financial advisors recommend the income replacement method anyway.

Key takeaways you should remember from this section are:

- Determining the face value of the policy is the last thing you should do when making life insurance decisions.
- The face value of your policy is dependent on what you want the money to do after you are gone.
- Don't forget that most of your expenses go away after you are gone.
- The face value should be the amount necessary for your loved ones to continue the same lifestyle they have now, after considering income, savings, and ongoing expenses.

OK, So you know how much life insurance is too much. Now you should figure out how much you actually need. Well, before we get there, you have to ask "what do I want my life insurance to accomplish?" Remember, it won't keep you alive and it isn't a measure of your wealth or value in the world. Life insurance does give your loved ones money after you die. They can use that money to maintain their lifestyle, or pay some expense that you would have paid if you didn't die. That's it, nothing more. So, first let's go through a list of hypothetical people and discuss their life insurance need:

- Freddy Grumpo makes $250,000 per year and has no friends and he doesn't like anyone. He doesn't need life insurance.
- Kyle Lazywitz has a job and sleeps on his parents sofa because he hasn't gotten around to getting an apartment. He isn't paying any expenses for his loved ones so he doesn't need life insurance.
- Carol Brady is a homemaker. Her husband financially supports her and their six kids. Although he is dependent on her for happiness and companionship, he is not financially dependent on her. She doesn't need life insurance. Her husband, Mike, does need life insurance.
- Betty White is 75 years old. She has a loving spouse, Biff, who does not work. They have several adult children, all with jobs. They have a few million dollars socked away from when she was a TV star. When she dies, Biff will inherit the money which is more than he can spend in his remaining life. Although he is financially dependent on her, he can use the inheritance to support himself and provide money to their children as needed. She doesn't need life insurance.
- Sally Workerbee is a single mother with a $250,000 outstanding balance on her mortgage. She has no savings. Her daughter is in Kindergarten. Her sister, who makes minimum wage, is the listed guardian of her daughter. Sally does need life insurance. She will need an amount to pay off her mortgage and provide her sister with enough money to support her daughter in the same lifestyle as her daughter is accustomed to.
- Sally's daughter is now 25 and is graduating law school. Sally exercised and ate right and didn't die. Sally's still has an outstanding mortgage of

$50,000. Sally doesn't need life insurance. If she dies, the house can be sold to pay the outstanding mortgage. The money left over (and her savings) can be left to her loved ones.
- Daddy Warbucks owns a closely held import / export company worth $25 million. Although his daughter had a hard knock life when she was younger, he expects she will be president of the company when he dies. He probably does need life insurance in order to pay estate taxes. This is a "death tax" imposed on the very wealthy (over $5.5 million in assets for singles, $11 million for married). If your wealth is less than that, don't worry about it.

So now, if you are still reading, it's time to figure out the life insurance product that is right for you. Here's our first definition – *term insurance*.

Term insurance – You pay a set annual premium every year for the entire term or until you die. If you die during the term, your beneficiaries get the face value of the policy; if you live until the end of the term or let the policy lapse, your beneficiaries get nothing.

There are several other types of life insurance, but they are generally not appropriate for 99% of the life insurance buying population. So figuring out the type of insurance you need is easy. You need term insurance. Fortunately for you this is the cheapest life insurance product out there. Unfortunately for you, the life insurance salesman you have an appointment with probably doesn't sell term insurance. She sells a different product that is higher cost and higher commission. That's OK. Cancel the appointment. You can buy term insurance online.

The next decision to make is how long should the term be. The longer the term is, the higher the premium will be per year. Also, the older you are, the higher the premium will be. So, knowing those two items, you need to pick a term equal to the time period you expect others to be financially dependent on your income (i.e. how long will you need life insurance).

There are several common life milestones that can cause someone to stop needing life insurance:

- Retirement – You don't have an income any more, so there is nobody who is dependent on your income any more.
- Kids get jobs and move out – They are no longer dependent on your income.
- You pay off the mortgage – Your spouse's expenses go down and now your kids have the income and savings to support their lifestyle without any help from you.
- You reach a savings goal that makes your family financially independent. Nobody is dependent on your income any more.
- Your spouse's income increases enough to support herself. Your spouse is no longer dependent on your income.
- You die.

Pick the longest possible time until the first of these milestones is expected to occur in your life. Be conservative, you don't want to be in a position to have to renew a life insurance policy when you are older and possibly less healthy than you are now.

OK, let's go back to the example of Sally Workerbee who we met earlier in the chapter. Ms. Workerbee is the only person discussed in that section who actually needed life insurance. Her need for life insurance is not permanent because she has confidence that her five year old daughter will become a productive, financially independent adult before she is 25 years old. In addition Ms. Workerbee is building up equity in her home which can be sold if she dies. By the time her daughter is 20, there will be over $200,000 in equity in Sally's home. This is certainly enough money to pay for her daughter's remaining education, and get her started in the world. Sally decides on a fifteen year term policy that will pay out benefits if Sally dies at any time before her daughter is 20 years old.

Key Takeaways for this section are:

- You probably should be looking for term insurance and should buy it online.
- You need to figure the longest possible time period that you will need life insurance. That should be your term.

Now that you've decided that you need term life insurance, and know the term you are going to select, it's time to figure out how much you actually need. Let's revisit Sally Workerbee from earlier. She is getting ready to go online and buy a term life insurance policy with a fifteen year term. She knows the cheapest time to buy life insurance is now. She is not getting any younger, and there is always a chance that she may develop a health condition in the future that will increase her premiums. She is going to pick a face value of the policy that is the maximum amount her beneficiaries could possibly need.

If she is to die, she would like for her daughter to continue to live in Sally's home, so she wants the policy to pay off her mortgage of $250,000.

Sally also wants her sister to maintain the same standard of living for her daughter. That's tough on a minimum wage job. Her sister will need extra money. Let's say Sally's current monthly budget is as follows:

Income	$5000
Taxes	$1000
Mortgage	$1250
Savings	$250
Lifestyle Expenses	$2500
Total Expenses	**$5000**

The only costs that must continue after Sally's death are some of the lifestyle expenses of $2500 / month. Sally's sister probably takes home about $1500 per month. Once Sally pays off the mortgage, Sally's sister can move into the house. If Sally can provide an additional $1000 /month to her sister, then her sister can maintain the same lifestyle. Sally will want to provide her sister this amount for at least fifteen years and possibly longer. Being that fifteen years is 180 months, the additional life insurance she will need to help her sister support the family lifestyle is 180 months x $1000 per month = $180,000. Sally's total life insurance need is:

Mortgage payment:
    $250,000

Funds to support lifestyle for 15 years:
    $180,000

Total:
    $430,000

Sally rounds the life insurance need up to $500,000. This allows her to leave some extra money to her sister. She goes online and confidently purchases a fifteen year term life insurance policy with a $500,000 face value. The cost turns out to be about $25 per month.

Yes, this is a high level presentation of the determination of a person's life insurance need. Hopefully it does provide you with a framework for you to determine your own life insurance need.

Key Takeaways for this section are:

- Financial advisors generally recommend purchasing too much life insurance.
- Life insurance is an important component of your finances.
- Everyone's life insurance needs are different.

Here's the cheat sheet for those of you who want to print out an outline of the life insurance buying process:

- Using the income replacement method to determine your life insurance need gets too big of a number.
- Many people don't need any life insurance.
- Of those who do, 99+% need only term insurance.
- Choose the appropriate term based on how long people will be financially dependent on your income.
- Choose the appropriate amount based on how much it will cost to pay for all of the expenses that are required for your dependents. Round up, just to be sure.
- Buy it online, it is probably cheaper.
- All life insurance is for is paying your outstanding expenses, and helping others maintain their lifestyle. That's it.
- Life insurance needs are independent of income.

Chapter 12 - Annuities

My definition of an annuity is:

<u>Annuity</u> - A financial product offering a very high commission to people who sell them.

Keep that definition in mind when considering purchasing an annuity. That's not to say that annuities are always bad and have no place in anyone's portfolio. However, it is to say that some advisors recommend annuities to people who don't need them because the temptation of a very high commission is too great for them to ignore.

A less controversial definition of an annuity is - a financial product that provides for a steady lifetime income in the future in exchange for a lump sum payment today. Social Security is very much like an inflation adjusted annuity in that it provides a lifetime payout in retirement in exchange for your social security contributions (taxes) today.

Fairly priced, that's a valuable service for retirees who want to make sure they don't outlive their money. Most annuities are not fairly priced because of the high commission charges embedded in the product.

Let's explore some events that can affect the value of an annuity to you:

You die sooner than expected. This one is pretty obvious. If you drop dead immediately after your purchase, you pretty much wasted your retirement savings. On the other hand, it didn't negatively impact your lifestyle because you didn't need the money anyway. You certainly shouldn't purchase an annuity if you have a reduced life expectancy compared to the average person.

Inflation is higher than expected. An issue with most annuities is that most annuities have fixed payments that do not adjust for inflation. An annuity that pays out $1000 per month today will still pay out $1000 per month in twenty years. However, the items you spend $1000 per month on today will cost you $1486 in twenty years if inflation is 2%, and $2119 per month if inflation is 4%. If you are expecting your savings to pay out the additional $486/mo required by your $1000/ month lifestyle and instead you have to come up with $1119 / mo from savings because inflation was higher than expected, you are likely to experience financial distress. The distress may come in the form of a lower lifestyle or a depleted savings account at some time in the future.

Investment returns are higher than expected. Every dollar you spend on an annuity is a dollar that you can't invest. If investment returns are stronger than expected, then the investment returns you would have earned will be higher than the income you receive from the annuity. Of course the point of an annuity is to protect you from the downside, not create a better upside to investing.

You develop a need for cash for a large expense. If you purchase an annuity, that lump sum is gone forever. Your ability to come up with a big pile of cash at a moment's notice is reduced by the cost of the annuity.

You are concerned that one day your ability to manage your retirement savings will disappear. Some people fear cognitive decline in their old age. This cognitive decline could affect one's ability to make intelligent investment decisions, often without the investor knowing it. If you purchase an annuity, the features of that annuity can protect you from making poor investment decisions into the future while still maintaining the lifestyle you paid for in your younger years.

Types of Annuities
There are several types of annuities to be aware of. The first category to be aware of is whether the annuity is immediate or deferred. All annuities are in one of these categories. An immediate annuity starts paying immediately. You pay your lump sum today, and then begin receiving monthly payments at the end of the month. This contrasts with a deferred annuity. A deferred annuity begins paying at a specific time in the future, often at age 65. If you die before then, you get nothing. Oh well, you didn't need the money for retirement anyway. I think of a deferred annuity as kind of like an insurance policy against living longer than expected.

The next category of features to consider is whether the annuity is fixed, variable, or indexed. A fixed annuity fixes the payments in the annuity contract.

You will get paid a fixed monthly payment as long as you live. Variable annuities are invested in mutual funds you select from those made available by the annuity provider. The monthly payment is calculated by formula based in part on the underlying value of the mutual funds you invested in. Often there is a minimum payment in order to preserve some income. Indexed annuities are similar except the formula is based on the performance of a stock index rather than a mutual fund. Indexed annuities usually have a cap and floor on how much the value of the annuity can change in a year.

Some annuities offer death benefits to heirs as well as the monthly payment to you while you are alive. If you wish to leave your heirs a death benefit (it's probably not necessary if you are retired), then it is best to buy a separate life insurance policy rather than an annuity with death benefits.

Some annuities offer "last to die" benefits as well. Last to die benefits are good for a married couple that requires an income for the rest of both of their lives. Please note that a married couple's monthly spending need decreases once the first spouse dies. Studies have shown that expenses go down by about 1/3 when the first death occurs. A good strategy it to purchase an annuity with last to die benefits for 1/3 of the spending need of the couple, and then purchase annuities without this benefit for each spouse also for 1/3 of the spending need of the couple. This strategy results in the couple receiving a payout of their full spending need as long as both are alive. Then, when the first spouse dies, the annuity payout reduces by 1/3 to adjust for the reduced spending need of the surviving spouse.

Inflation protection is a critical feature of an annuity and unfortunately many annuity providers are either not providing that protection or providing it at a very high cost. As mentioned earlier, the risk to your finances from higher than expected inflation is about as significant as the risk from a longer than expected lifespan. I would not purchase an annuity without inflation protection.

Income Tax for Annuities
If you do purchase an annuity, it will be taxed somewhat favorably-- initially. The IRS performs a calculation where it divides the annuity purchase price by the expected annuity payments. This percentage of annuity payment is not taxable income. The remainder of the annuity payment is taxable.

But there's a catch. If you live longer than expected, your entire annuity payment becomes taxable. That's because payments beyond your expected lifespan are considered to be a profit on the annuity. The result is that a significant part of your annuity income is not taxable in early retirement, but in late retirement annuity income and taxable income will increase.

Calculating the value of an annuity is a complex actuarial calculation involving many assumptions including expected lifespan, expected interest rates, and expected investment returns. While performing an actuarial calculation of the value of an annuity is beyond the scope of this book, I can provide you with a few rules of thumb to think about:

- A healthy 60 to 65 year old can expect to live twenty more years; however, you should expect to live thirty more years because it would be a bummer to run out of retirement savings when you are in your 80's and still have ten years left to live.
- The rule of thumb for safe withdrawal rates of invested retirement assets is 4% per year. Recently some investment advisers have challenged that withdrawal rate as too aggressive in light of the very low interest rates currently offered; several advisers suggest that 3.6% is a more appropriate withdrawal rate.
- When considering the value and appropriateness of an annuity to you, don't forget about Social Security's contribution to your retirement. For a high earner waiting until age 70 to begin collecting social security, a monthly benefit of $2500 to $3000 is typical. You can contact the Social Security Administration to find out the anticipated benefit for you. (Social Security is not going to stop paying out benefit checks any time soon despite what you hear; There is expected to be enough money in the trust fund right now to pay out all benefit checks in full until 2034;

after that point there will be enough to pay out 80% of benefits for the indefinite future.
- Annuities are a good addition to the portfolio of someone who can just barely afford retirement. It changes the retirement planning thought process from "I think I can afford to retire if everything goes according to plan over the next twenty years" to "I can afford retirement". Of course the value of an annuity to your heirs is zero so the purchase of an annuity decreases any inheritance.
- If you are heading towards a retirement savings that is signficantly under your retirement need, then an annuity is not right for you. You should keep your money invested and hope for the best. Maybe you'll die early; maybe investment returns will be great and will provide you the income you need after all. At least you've got a shot at a good retirement. An annuity in this case would lock in an income that is inadequate and guarantee your failure to meet your retirement income goals.
- If you have more than enough even under the most conservative scenarios, then an annuity is not right for you either. Keep your money invested; you know that no matter what you'll have enough. In addition, if returns work out in your favor, you can generate a significant upside for your heirs.

Chapter 13 - I'm Going to Open My Own Business

Many people with this dream think of opening their own business this way:

Hooray, I've dilligently saved money so I can get out of the rat race. Now I'm going to put my money down, get a small business loan and open my own shop somewhere and do what I've always loved and follow my bliss. After all, I'm a great cook, so my restaurant is a guaranteed success.

Instead of this way:

Hooray I've diligently saved money for my future and I now have the opportunity to invest in a new business venture. The leader of the business I am going to invest in is thinly capitalized and not experienced in running the business. In addition to my investment, the business will also borrow money at unfavorable interest rates. The business is in a very competitive industry. I've looked at the numbers and found that if the business is not profitable within twelve months, it will have to close. If the business closes, I will lose 100% of my investment. In addition, I may also be required to pay back the loans the business took out. Also, the business will require a very significant time investment. If the business succeeds, I will earn about the same amount of money as I did before I invested in the business.

I'm not saying don't follow your bliss and open that beach bar or bed & breakfast. What I am saying is don't think that paying money to follow your bliss is anything remotely resembling an investment. Money or time spent following your bliss is a luxury, not an investment. Before you put your money down on following your bliss, make sure you have enough left over so that you will still be able to achieve your financial goals and retirement need. Don't despair if you can't do both. With each passing year, your financial situation will improve (if you stick to your plan). It is possible that a few years in the future you will have the money to follow your bliss and have a secure retirement. Now that's a great position to be in.

Learn how to run a business by first running a business you have some knowledge about.
Many people have the dream of owning their own business, being their own boss, and creating something of their own. However, no job prepares you for owning your own dream business better than actually owning a business, any business. If I were opening a new restaurant and had to choose between a great chef and the owner of a successful landscaping business to partner with me on the new restaurant, I would choose the business owner. We might hire the chef, though.

You see, owning a business requires you to know a little about all aspects of the business, rather than a lot about one aspect of the business. A business owner needs to know how to market and sell their product; a business owner needs to know how to price their product and control expenses; a business owner needs to know how to hire the right people; and of course, a business owner needs to know how to deliver a great product. If a business owner fails in any of these areas, the business will fail. While the chef will know how to deliver a great product, the chef will likely not have any skill in the other areas of business management. That's why I would rather partner with the owner of the landscaping business and hire the chef.

Step 1 towards owning your own dream business is experience in owning and running a business. It sounds kind of like a circular no win situation, but you can make it work.

Before you begin running your dream business, you need to become educated on how to be a successful business owner. The best way to educate yourself is to just do it. Baseball players don't take classes on how to hit a baseball, they just practice. Concert pianists don't take classes on how to play better, they just practice. The same is true for successful business owners. Consider the cost of financing your first business as your cost of education.

With this thought in mind, find a way to buy or form your own business for as little money as possible. If you have to change or quit your job to run this business, consider your lost earnings as part of the cost. Once you've decided on the way to go, go for it! Remember this isn't your dream business, this is school. Run the business with the goal of making it successful.

Over time one of a few things will happen:

1. You decide you don't want to own a business after all. There's too many aspects to running a business that you just don't like. If that's the case, sell the business and recommit to your old job. You won't feel bad, though, because you won't have to go through the rest of your life thinking "I wish I opened my own business".
2. You realize you have grown to love this business and develop more skill at running it each day. You decide to continue on with the business you are in.
3. You make some mistakes, learn from them, and make better business decisions over time. You develop an exit plan for your current business. Based on your experience with this business, you are able to make an intelligent plan for your dream business. You'll make much smarter decisions from the outset. You'll know how much money you'll need to start, and you'll be on a much better path to make it happen. Once you have saved your starting capital which is above and beyond your retirement savings, you can go for it.
4. You fail. Nope. That can't happen with this plan. Either you succeed, you educate yourself on how to succeed, or your goals change to something new you are passionate about.

Those are the only three things that can happen.

Chapter 14 - First Steps for Aspiring Business Owners

How to look at the Investment

When you are looking to buy a business, make sure you are not just buying a job. What I mean by that is that you should make sure that your income as a business owner is higher than it would be if you were doing the same job as an employee of someone else's business. If it isn't higher, then it means you are getting an income as an employee and your business is not making money at all. Or more simply, you made an investment that isn't generating any return at all.

To make an intelligent business purchase, you need to compare the your financial situation without the purchase to the situation after the purchase.

Without the purchase, you get investment gains from the money-- use 15% or 20% per year for a high risk investment such as a small business; you also get income from your job. A 15% return is much higher than what you can expect from the stock market. However, 15% is appropriate in this calculation because of the risk.

If you earn $70K per year and you are considering purchasing a business for $100K, and running the business full time, your annual profit must be the required $15K gain + $70K lost earned income = $85K-- just to break even. If you can't reasonably expect to make at least $85K per year profit from this business based on your understanding of the expected revenues and expenses, then your business purchase will be harming your overall financial situation. Before you purchase the business, you must make sure the purchase is something you can afford.

How to get the money
You do not get the money from your IRA. At every small business expo or franchise show I have ever been to there has always been some huckster pitching a new business structure or legal maneuver that will allow you to use your IRA to finance your business purchase. Don't be fooled. This is definitely not a good idea, and is probably illegal. See Chapter 6 for more information on that.

Get the money from your savings, get the money by remortgaging your house if you have home equity, get friends and family to invest or lend you the money. If that's not enough, there may be one more reasonable strategy available.

Get the money from someone you don't even know -- the person who wants to sell the business to you. After all, they are on your side. They also want you to be able to come up with the money to buy their business. Offer the seller 25% to 50% of the price of the business in cash. Then offer the remainder of the sales price, and a little more as an annual payment out of profits over the next three to seven years.

So a sample offer might be worded like this: "I know you want $100K for your business. I agree that price is fair. After all it generates a $20K per year profit. I will pay you $30K today; in addition, I will pay you $17K per year for the next five years. I'll get the money out of the business profit. If I miss a payment, you keep the $30K and all of the annual payments previously made, and you get the business back." This offer can be a real win-win.

- You get a $100K business for only $30K.
- After 5 years you get all of the profit.
- Whenever it's time to sell the business, you get the entire value of the business even though you put up only $30K.
- If the business turns out to be a dog, you get to give it back with no further obligation. Instead of being out $100K, you only lose a fraction of the amount.

It's a great deal from the seller's viewpoint as well.

- The seller gets to sell the business right away to someone who might not otherwise be able to buy the business.
- The seller actually gets $30K +$85K = $115K ($17K x 5 yrs = $85K). This is actually higher than the $100K asking price.
- There's a chance that the seller will be getting some money to take a vacation and will actually get his business back at some point in the future.

Deals like the above are reasonably common. For a deal like this to work, the seller must be confident that the current profit will be sustainable under new ownership. The seller also must be confident in your ability to generate profits for the business at least as well as she did. That's great! Because you, as a buyer, want the seller to feel that way. The seller's willingness to do a deal like that is a vote of confidence in you and the business.

How to get customers

Advertising and sales is probably the most neglected part of a business for people who are following their bliss by opening their own business. When I encourage new business owners to spend more on advertising, I get one of three responses:

"I'll advertise when I get more clients." Wrong. A business is an investment and business expenses are often investments in the future. You should have your vision of how big you are looking for your business to be in the short / medium term. Now advertise as if you already have that client base. Your prospects want to choose a successful business to buy from. You must act the part. Show them that you are successful by advertising like a successful business. Your prospects will notice that.

"I'm the best at what I do. People will find me." Your prospects don't know who you are. When your prospects are looking for a new business to buy from, they don't just know you are out there. They find businesses through word of mouth or some sort of

advertising. When you open your own business, your word of mouth benefit starts out at zero, so you better advertise.

"It doesn't work, or it costs too much." Sadly, this one is true. 90% of all spending on advertising is a waste. However 10% of advertising spending generates an excellent return and makes up for all of the waste. You've got to start advertising right away so you can start to identify all of the different types of advertising that are a waste of money to you. Eventually you'll find an advertising initiative that doesn't turn out to be a waste. It will actually deliver lots of customers to you. So go out and get busy wasting money on advertisements. Eventually you will fail at wasting money and get lots of clients.

Keeping the books
Yes, do that regularly, every month at the least. In addition to the fact that it is required in order to accurately fill out tax forms, it is also necessary to keep and review the books to know if you are making money and identify ways to improve your profitability even further. Keeping the books is not only about writing down all of your revenue and expenses; it is also about recording your profitability (revenue - expenses) and profit margin (profitability / revenue) over time and track how these values are changing. You can use this information to know if your business is heading in the right direction.

Basic personal finance software (like Quicken) can help you. If you are scared of computers, you can even do it in a ledger book like they did in the old days. While Quicken is my choice, a ledger book is great too, if that will motivate you to start.

Chapter 15 - Combining Finances with Your Significant Other

At some point in our lives there comes a time where we decide to merge our life with someone else. Oftentimes when this happens we decide to go all in and merge all of our lives, including our financial life. By the way, I am not just talking spouse or significant other. Sometimes if you are the caretaker of your parents, you may be sharing a financial life with them. Or sometimes parents merge finances with their adult kids.

Merging financial lives is fine, if that's what you want. It shows a full commitment to the relationship. Great! But merge finances with someone with your eyes wide open. Know what you are getting into. Just like you want to know what you are getting into before you commit.

When you get to the point where you are considering merging finances with another person, you should agree with that other person that your finances should be an open book. You should share information about income, expenses, assets, debts, credit rating, and reasonably foreseeable changes to those items. You should expect to have this information shared with you. As you know, after you merge finances, you are responsible for all debts and expenses that either of you take on. Like I said before, make sure you know what you are getting into.

Next, you should have some discussion on how the future income and expenses will be divided after your finances are merged. Things like who pays the rent, how your student loan gets repaid, what your savings can be used for, and more broadly, what level of financial lifestyle you should live. (Of course your lifestyle should be less than your combined income, but how much less is what you need to discuss).

Make sure you are on the same page. If your thoughts on expenses and savings aren't reasonably close, you probably shouldn't share finances.

Now the act of actually combining finances is tricky. So my suggestion is to not jump into it. Combine finances as the need arises. You may find over time that sharing a financial life together does not necessarily mean merging all financial accounts. As a matter of fact, of all of our financial accounts, my wife and I have only one joint account. We both contribute to it as we are able. Each of us has a checkbook, and we agree to write checks only for large joint expenses. We shredded the ATM card the bank sent in the mail. Every surprise windfall of money either of us receives {e.g. consulting assignment) goes into this account. Every surprise expense comes out of this account {e.g. car accident). Whenever we write checks from the joint account, we tell the other about the check immediately.

My wife and I each manage our own personal bank accounts and credit cards. Each of us agree on a monthly personal budget. Any take home income that is more than that budgeted amount is deposited in the joint account. If one of us doesn't have the income to support their monthly personal budget, the joint account can transfer money to make up for the shortfall.

It's a great system for us. We both know exactly what is going on. Part of the reason we know what is going on in our joint account is because so few transactions are in that account. However the few transactions that are in that account are the big ones. For us, they account for about 1/3 of all of our family spending. Just by setting things up that way, each of us has very detailed knowledge of 2/3 of the family budget (personal spending and the joint account spending). We will never wonder where all the money went. I specifically know about 2/3 of the budget, and I also know that my wife spends about the same amount as me on her personal life. That seems fair to me-- I don't need any more details than that. What an argument saver! I don't want to know that my wife spends $200 on haircuts before she screams at me for not noticing how nice her hair looks after the haircut.

Book 5 – Extra Credit – Money for Fun

Chapter 1 - What Would You Do if You Had $1,000,000

Having a million dollars shouldn't be viewed as a fantasy. It should be viewed as part of your long-term plan. If you have at least a middle class income and want to retire before you are 70 or so, you'll probably need to save about a million dollars to maintain your lifestyle. So this isn't a fantasy question, this is a question that you need to answer so that you'll know what to do when you get there.

First, let me give you comfort that it's really easy to get there:

- My financial calculator says that if you save $10K / yr for 30 yrs. at a 7% investment return rate, you'll get to $1M. In other words, a family with a $70K income should live a $60K lifestyle.
- If that sounds too hard, you can start out saving only $7063 per year if you promise to increase your savings with inflation.
- Or how about saving as little as $4076 per year if you expect to earn 10% per year on your investments and will increase your contribution with inflation.
- Or finally, if you are young enough, and can save for 40 years, you need only $1929 per year with a 10% return and can increase contributions with inflation.

The point is, a million dollars is very doable.

In your mind you should change the chapter title to "What Will You Do When You Have a Million Dollars?" First, keep in mind that people almost never actually "have" $1M as in "Look over on the kitchen table. I counted that money. It's a million dollars." No, a million dollars generally arrives over time without much fanfare at all.

For me it went like this. I was paying bills and balancing my checkbook on Quicken like I do at the beginning of every month. I clicked the "update" button which updates the value of all my online bank accounts as well as stock and mutual fund prices. After all of the account values were updated , I looked to the bottom of the screen and noticed that the net worth was calculated at $1,006,432.10 (don't actually remember the last few digits). So there it was. I spent the next 30 minutes paying the bills and my day was pretty much ordinary.

A million dollars in net worth is generally scattered among several different accounts, some IRAs and 401(k)s, maybe some home equity, etc. In other words, a million dollarsin net worth is really quite abstract. The key here is a million dollars is really far beyond any need for your day to day cash flow, or an emergency fund. As I mentioned in the chapter about $100K, you should already have an investment account. However, as you approach a million dollars in net worth, different issues become important.

Once you start approaching a million dollars in net worth, the smartest thing you can do in managing your personal finances is to **not do anything stupid with your personal finances.** Commit to learning how to determine a good investment / financial opportunity from a bad one. This skill will be worth thousands of dollars to you over the course of your life.

The second most important thing you can do at this level of wealth is making sure that your wealth is diversified.

Arguably, diversification of assets is something that should be done right away, as soon as you have enough money to begin investing. However, as your wealth increases, diversification takes on increasing importance. Diversification of assets sounds much more complicated than it really is. It just means that your investments should be spread around so that no single event, or bad stock market day can significantly impact your net worth. In layman's terms it means "don't keep all your eggs in one basket". You aren't diversified if you have a substantial percentage of your investment money in a single stock, or even a single type of stock (e.g. technology, small cap). If you've been moving forward your whole life making smart personal finance decisions, diversification has likely come about naturally. Some of your money is likely in cash in the form of an emergency fund. An additional portion of your net worth is likely in the form of home equity. You've likely been contributing to an

IRA and/or a 401(k) and used those investment dollars to buy some sort of diverse stock fund. As your wealth grows, you should acknowledge that a portion of your money should be outside of the stock market altogether-- you should have some money in bond funds, CDs, and cash above your emergency fund needs. Great! You are diversified.

There actually is quite a bit more analytic effort that can be applied to the effort of diversification. Many financial planners, including me, decide on a target percentage of assets in a wide variety of categories-- US stocks, fixed income, international, etc. Every month or so I look at my investments updated value and calculate the percentage of my investments in each investment category. If the target percentage is lower than the actual percentage for an investment category, then I know that I should think about selling something in that investment category and using the proceeds to buy into an underrepresented investment category. You can learn more about recommended percentages elsewhere. The point is you can make sure your portfolio is diversified. You don't need someone else's help if you are willing to spend the effort on educating yourself.

As your wealth level moves through six and towards seven figures, you start to get exposure to many more financial investments. "Financial Advisers" start sending you letters and calling you on the phone offering to explain some new financial products that are perfectly suited to you (in their opinion). In addition, some financial coaches and advisers (maybe me), will contact you to offer financial planning services. Some of these services may even be touted as "free" services.

I'm sure your mom told you at least once that nothing in life is free; dad probably told you that "there's no such thing as a free lunch." Financial products and services are not an exception to that rule. However, providers of financial products and services are much better at hiding the costs of these services from you. You see, your cost for these services is paid through three channels. First is the direct cost that you pay for the product. You know about this cost because you had to write a check to the provider. The second is the cost to the financial adviser to compensate him for his analysis of your financial situation and his recommendations to you. This cost is sometimes, but not always zero. You will know this cost as well, because you will have to write a check, or sign an authorization for him to withdraw that amount from your investment account.

The third cost is most important, because it is often the largest. It is also the cost that is least obvious. This cost is the expenses that are taken from your investment on a regular basis. These expenses are designed to compensate the professionals for investing your money as well as the advisers that ~~sold you~~ advised you to buy the investment. These expenses lower the value of your investment and reduce your future financial return. Most investment products remove expenses quarterly or annually for as long as you own the investment. A high expense product might have *10 times* the expenses removed from your investment compared to a low expense product. This expense differential, combined with the associated lost investment gain on the removed expenses can amount to tens of thousands of dollars for a $100K investment held long term. Usually there is no difference in the performance of the underlying financial product.

So you need to be able to identify the difference between a high expense and a low expense product. Below are details on how to determine the exact amount of these expenses.

You can usually find out a fund's expenses online on the fund's website. If you can't, you can definitely find a fund's expenses in the fund's prospectus. As an example, that the "Acquired Fund Fees and Expenses" for the Vanguard S&P 500 Index Fund is 0.14%. That's great. There are some mutual funds charging expense ratios as high as 1.5%– That means the fees they are getting from you to manage your money are more than 10 times higher. You definitely want to look at your mutual funds to be sure they are low cost mutual funds.

Part 2 of your quest to lower your expenses is to cut out or at least reduce the commissions you pay the middleman. You don't need to pay any commissions on mutual funds. Choose a no-load mutual fund from the many fund offerings online and you'll be all set.

If you are going to buy stocks or ETFs (you generally don't need to, as mutual funds effectively deliver the upside of the stock market, while reducing the downside through diversification), buy stocks through a low cost broker. There are many brokerages with trading commissions under $15 per trade. If you are paying more than that, you are flushing money down the toilet.

Chapter 2 - Lending

Earlier in this book series I devoted a chapter to borrowing. Borrowing is something that should only occur earlier in your adult life when you are investing in your education and your home. It is interesting that many of the big expenses in life are front loaded to your early adulthood when your income, your savings, and your ability to borrow at favorable interest rates are all reduced. Early adulthood has the costs of your education, your first home, your first car, your furniture, and possibly expenses related to getting married and parenting. The chapter on borrowing discussed how you should borrow to pay for your life only when you absolutely have to. Probably the only borrowing that you absolutely need to do is borrowing for a home. The reason why you need to limit borrowing in your early adulthood is that you want to begin saving and investing as soon as possible. Getting rid of debt allows you to build an emergency fund and investment portfolio sooner rather than later.

Eventually your financial position will likely become secure enough where you can afford to lend money to someone who is seeking to borrow money. Your possible borrowers fall into one of several categories:

1. A stranger. Peer to peer lending is a fancy way to say that you are lending money to a stranger that you don't know very much about. The lure is that these strangers will promise to pay you back at a very high

interest rate (over 10%). The downside is that you don't know very much about the borrower, and you really have no idea if they will pay you back. The peer to peer loan broker (e.g. Lending Club) will be no help to you because they get paid when you lend the money, and they don't lose money if the borrower defaults. So, the loan broker will do everything they can to get you to lend the money, then they will take their cut, and laugh all the way to the bank. It's a really bad deal for you, so don't do this.

2. A bank. When you get a CD, you are essentially lending money to the bank. It's very secure because even if the bank goes under, the FDIC insurance will step in and pay your CD. The downside is that the interest rates are very low. They are generally only 0.25% or so better than an ordinary savings account.

3. A large corporation or government. When you buy a bond, you are essentially lending money to the issuer of that bond. You earn a considerably higher interest rate when buying a bond. Unfortunately, you need to pay a commission to a bond broker and that commission will eat into your return. In addition, you run the risk that the issuer of the bond will not have the money to pay you back. A less risky and more cost efficient way to buy bonds is through a bond fund (a mutual fund that invests in bonds). Make sure to choose a bond fund with low expenses and no load. Reread the chapter on investments if you need to. A bond fund has the advantage of diversification. If an issuer doesn't pay back the money it owes, your

investment is not wiped out because the bond fund you invested in has hundreds or maybe even thousands of issuers. The interest rate on bond funds are higher than different bonds, but there is a chance that the value of your bond fund will go down if interest rates rise after you buy the fund. Over a multi year period, though, it is very unlikely that you will lose money.

4. A trusted friend or relative in a financial jam. This is the person that calls you and asks if she can come over and discuss something important. The discussion usually involves your friend telling you a long confusing story. While you don't really understand all of the details of the story, your friend makes it perfectly clear that she needs money and it's not her fault. She then tells you she wants to borrow money. Lending a friend money is like paying to lose a friendship. Your friend has put you in a tough spot. You should always say "No," to the loan request. Don't lend the money. If you really want to help your friend out, gift your friend the money.

If you have a friend who is in a financial jam and is asking you for money knowing that borrowing from a friend can end a friendship, then they are desperate, or they are not really your friend. Either way, you shouldn't lend money to this person. Gift a friend the money if money can really get your friend out of this jam. Don't lend this friend the money. Your friend is already under stress. She already can't support her lifestyle. She definitely won't be able to support her lifestyle if she has a loan payment to you on top of her current expenses. And to top it all off she likely has no savings and poor credit. If she had savings or good credit, she never would have asked you for the money. She would have borrowed from the bank.

Why lend money to someone who almost certainly won't be able to pay it back? You are setting yourself up for disappointment, setting your friend up for the additional stress of trying to pay back the loan to you, and you are setting your friendship up for ruin because of the stress and disappointment caused by the failed loan. Don't lend the money. If you can afford to gift the money then do that, and feel good about it.

5. Somebody with a business idea. The somebody may be a friend, family member, or acquaintance. It doesn't matter, the analysis of this is the same. There is no "sure thing" business idea. New businesses, especially new small businesses are very risky. Often in a few years they run out of money and go bankrupt. While the business idea may sound very promising, you should keep in mind that every new business has a significant possibility of going bankrupt. Just think about the restaurants in your town. How often do they last more than three years? Not that often, right? Now remember that all of those restaurants were promising business ideas that people poured money and energy into.

So if you have a reasonably possible chance of losing 100% of your money helping a business get off the ground, you need to have a significant upside to make the investment worthwhile. A loan offering a 5% or even 10% interest rate isn't worth that kind of risk. No, if you want to invest in this business idea, you should demand to own a percentage of the company. Once you own part of the business, you become entitled to a share of the profits, and a share of the proceeds whenever the business sells. Typically, your ownership stake should be something close to the percentage of your investment relative to the total startup investment of the business.

In other words, if you invest $50,000 in your friend's restaurant, and he invests $100,000. You should demand a 1/3 ownership stake, and therefore be entitled to 1/3 of the profits. Sure, you can still go bankrupt under this arrangement, but you can also get a significant upside if the business becomes successful and starts generating profits. If you are not confident the business will earn a suitable profit to make it worthwhile for you (I'd probably want about $10K profit share per year on my $50K investment...), then this isn't the investment for you. You should pass. If you do invest, make sure you have a lawyer draw up documents reflecting the investment. Remember the guys who said they invested in Facebook but couldn't prove it. That little mistake cost them billions of dollars.

6. A trusted young adult friend or relative needing money to invest in herself. You may know a young adult that needs to pay for college or a home, or other expenses relating to getting adulthood up and

running. This young adult should have a secure job that can comfortably pay off any loan you might give them. If you have the asset level where the loan is a reasonably small investment for you (certainly under 1/3 of your assets), then this can be a win-win. Interest rates that lenders charge for a mortgage or a personal loan are much higher than a worthwhile interest rate for you to charge. The reason why it is worth it for you to charge a lower interest rate is that you can charge an interest rate higher than a CD or bond fund would pay you (1% to 2%) while still being lower than what the banks will charge to your younger friend (4% to 6%). In other words if your lend money to your trusted young adult, and charge 3.5%, you'll be very happy because you won't be able to get 3.5% anywhere else. Your trusted young adult will be happy because the interest rate he has to pay you is lower than it would be anywhere else. Make sure you make the agreement in writing so everyone is on the same page. Also make sure you know the young adult's income so you can be sure he can afford your loan payment.

7. Somebody else with a convincing story. No way, don't lend the money. The group of people falling into the "somebody else" category include "down on their luck" people that have run into financial problems through no fault of their own. They include friends of friends with business ideas, etc. People who say they are going to come into money "soon", and basically everyone else looking for money who doesn't fall into one of the six categories above. Remember, there are

businesses that have the sole purpose of evaluating the likelihood of a loan getting paid back. These businesses will lend money to whoever is likely to be successful in making the loan payments. The fact someone is coming to you rather than a bank probably means that the bank's loan experts believe the loan will likely not be repaid. Trust their judgment, you shouldn't lend the money either.

Chapter 3 - Set for Life

This was originally the "What Would You Do If You Won The Lottery" chapter. Then I reminded myself that I don't want to encourage buying lottery tickets (even though I do buy them sometimes). But more importantly I don't want you to feel that becoming set for life is an implausible fantasy; on the contrary, becoming set for life is totally within your control. Earn more, spend less. Invest the difference. Don't make any dumb mistakes. You'll definitely get there.

In most careers, from skilled labor to professional level jobs, highly experienced people get paid between 2x and 3x what entry level employees do. Now here's the thing, many people recall their early young adult life as among the happiest times of their life. If you are a young adult, keep that in mind as well.

So if you triple the income of a happy person, that person does not need to spend their income gain-- they are already happy. When income triples, much of the income gain can be banked and ultimately invested.

For me, and this is just my personal issue, I have always had a strong drive towards a particular spending need. I have always wanted to be "set for life". To me, being set for life means being able to spend at a level that can deliver my happiness for the rest of my life even if my income drops to zero. This gives me the freedom of not being dependent on any boss, job, or even career. In this scenario, I only have to work when I am doing something enjoyable (like writing this book). Of course anyone set for life, especially someone relatively young, is going to engage in something financially productive during much of their lives. So being set for life requires a slightly smaller financial nest egg than it would if you required income for life. I suppose if you didn't find any activity that had value as enjoyable, then you would need a nest egg equal to your set for life nest egg, but that's more of a topic for a self help book.

Calculating how much money you need to have saved up to be set for life is beyond the scope of this chapter. This calculation, though, should be done if you have the goal of being set for life. If you aren't comfortable with going through the minute details of such an analysis, you should pay someone to do that for you. It's pretty hard to achieve a savings goal if you have no idea how to tell when you get there.

What is 'Set for Life'?
I can help you get started with the calculation, though. Here's a few things to consider.

Your "set for life" expenses are not the same as your current income. The biggest adjustment is for you to distinguish income from spending. You can do this by looking at the outflows of your bank account. Now take away income tax payments, job related expenses, retirement contributions, and savings account contributions, all of these outflows will go away when you are set for life. Also take away debt payments. You are going to pay them off before you are set for life. The remainder is your net spending. Figure out your monthly net spending.

On top of your net spending, you probably should add 5% to 10% to account for emergency spending or "one time spending". I am going to call that your "net-plus" spending.

Figuring out your "set for life" nest egg involves first figuring out how much money you need to be set for life "pre-retirement" and how much you need "post-retirement". A "set for life" person claims social security at age 70 because that is the age where your social security benefit maxes out.

Set for Life Pre-Retirement

You know exactly how many years your pre-retirement will last. Pre retirement is from now to age 70.

The first thing you must do when you become set for life is to pay off all your debts, mortgage, student loan, car loan, everything.

If you are around 45 years old, multiply your net plus spending by 200. That will support you for about 25 years. Yup, 200 months savings supports you for 300 months (25 years) because of all your investment gains. If you are 45, you need 200 months spending after paying off all your debts for your pre-retirement set for life nest egg.

If you are closer to 30 years old, multiply your net plus spending number by 250. That will support you for about 40 years! That's even more amazing. An extra 50 months savings can support you for an extra 15 years.

Now for fun, multiply your net plus spending by 300. That will support you forever-- you will be able to pay for your lifestyle with your investment gains alone. If you have 300 months spending already, you don't need to do any more calculations. You are set for life.

Set for Life Post-Retirement

When you are set for life, you expect your retirement to last a really long time. Your Social Security benefit will help, but it generally won't be enough. You can get an exact projection of your monthly social security benefit through the Social Security website (ssa.gov), but if you are too lazy to do that, you can estimate. Social Security generally pays about 1/4 of your average salary during your working years if you retire early. It will pay less if you retire very early (before age 40).

So, once you've estimated your social security benefit, subtract it from your net plus spending. Now multiply this reduced amount by 200 to 250 (depending on whether you want to save for a 95 year lifespan or a 110 year lifespan). This is your post-retirement nest egg.

Of course you don't need your post-retirement nest egg until you reach retirement when you are 70. You can put aside a lot less money now because your post retirement nest egg will grow over the few decades between now and age 70. You can discount that post retirement nest egg because it is so far into the future.

Divide by 2 if you are about 50 years old.

Divide by 3 if you are about 38 years old.

Divide by 4 if you are about 30 years old.

This discounted number is how much you need to have today for your post retirement nest egg.

The Answer
Your "set for life" number is equal to your debts plus your pre-retirement nest egg plus your post retirement nest egg.
The calculations outlined above give you a quick approximation of how much money you need to be set for life. Obviously you should have a more detailed calculation performed by an expert before you quit your job. The point of the calculation described above is to give you an idea of the target nest egg you should be striving for as well as help you understand the enormous value of investing your money early.

My recommendation is for you to continue updating your estimate of your set for life number. Once your actual nest egg starts to get close to your set for life number, you can bring in a financial planner to help you with a more refined estimate so you can make sure you are on the right track.

Chapter 4 - What Would You Do If You Won the Lottery?

This is the final chapter, and I think the most fun, in the exploration of dealing with increasing amounts of wealth. We started with $1000, and then progressed one zero at a time past one million, and then up to "set for life". All of the prior chapters were designed to prepare you for all of those eventualities. If you manage your finances intelligently, you'll definitely make it to "set for life" eventually.

Yes, you'll definitely get there. If you look left as you step out into the street and see an out of control pickup truck racing towards you, you become set for life at that moment. Your goal, of course, is to be set for life for as long a time period as possible instead of for the one second between the moment you see the pickup and the moment it knocks you into the afterlife.

Anyway, this chapter is more of a fun exercise in handling a fantasy. The exercise helps you spend more time in thinking and learning about how to manage your ever increasing wealth. It's probably also fun to be an expert at cocktail parties in discussing the management of lottery winnings.

Step 1 - Don't Lose Your Ticket So, you found out you won. Sign your ticket. Take a picture of you and your ticket. Save it on your computer, and upload it to the cloud. Put your ticket in a safe place.

Step 2 - Prepare to Make Your Claim Tell your spouse. Your ticket is community property even if you bought it. Don't think you can claim the prize, divorce your spouse, and keep the money. Somebody already tried that and the divorce court wasn't impressed. The judge called the lottery winnings a "concealed asset". The judge awarded the ticket to the spouse it was concealed from. The actual lottery winner got nothing. Other than your spouse, tell as few people as possible.

Plan your trip to lottery headquarters in the state capital as soon as possible. Be prepared to change your contact information especially if you win one of the big jackpots. Lottery winners names and addresses are public information.

Step 3 - Decide on What Experts You are Going to Need to Help You. I've heard some people say you should surround yourself with a team of experts before claiming your money- They say you need a financial planner, a lawyer, and a CPA at a minimum. I disagree. Acquire your expertise and financial team as needed. If you do it that way, you'll be better equipped to select the right expert for you. So, for now, it's just you, your spouse, and your ticket.

Step 4 - Your First Financial Decision - Lump Sum or Annual Payments. Powerball will take out the first 25% of your check to pay towards income taxes (lottery winnings are taxable). They send you a check for the remaining 75%.

So, if you win a $10M Powerball Jackpot, there's $7.5M after taxes. Then they reduce this number again to account for their lost income from giving you a lump sum now. If they were able to spread their payments to you over thirty years, they could invest that money for a few decades and earn a great deal of interest. They reduce their payout to you to discourage you from taking the lump sum. The lottery guys estimate that they would earn $2.23M in investment income if they got to hold onto the money. As a result they are taking that $2.23M out of your winnings. You get the rest – $5.27M.

"Well," you complain ungratefully, "I don't want to lose half my winnings before I even get my hands on it. I'll take the annual payments." Annual payments also end up being a lot less than you think. Your first payment on your $10M winnings will be a measly $112,885.77– barely over 1% of the jackpot. "Why is it so small," you ungratefully wonder. "I thought winning a $10M jackpot would lead to champagne and caviar, not an ordinary upper middle class lifestyle."

Here's how they calculate your first paycheck. First, they take out 25% of the payment in taxes, of course. Next, the lottery commission has decided that it is most beneficial to lottery winners if their annual payment increases over time to account for inflation and their increasingly extravagant lifestyle. So, the lottery commission adjusts its first annual payment downward so that it can afford to give you a 5% raise every year throughout the thirty lottery payments.

That increase starts to get very significant over time. Your tenth payment will be about $175K, your twentieth payment will be about $285K, and your thirtieth (final) payment will be $465K. They've done the math. It all adds up to the same $7.5M after tax number used in the lump sum calculations.

So, both options are a lot less awesome than initially expected, but which is the better of the two? In my opinion, in almost all cases, the lump sum is the better deal. While the lottery guys take $2.23 million of your money when you select the lump sum, You can easily make that money back by investing the part of your lump sum that you are not spending right away.

I recently performed a simple analysis that concluded that you could make the same exact annual payments to yourself as the lottery commission and still have money left over at the end of the 30 years if you invest the remainder and get an investment return of at least 2.06% per year. That's a pretty low bar to meet. The stock market earns between 7% and 10% per year over the long term. Your investments will probably earn a return in that neighborhood.

A more detailed analysis would have to consider your risk tolerance as well as the effect of investment taxes on the result. While everyone has a different situation with regard to these items, consideration of these items generally push up the required investment return to somewhere between 3.5% and 4.0% This should still be easily doable over the long term. So, more likely than not, lottery winners should take the lump sum.

The few exceptions are: 1) people who are already quite wealthy and would invest their winnings in conservative assets, and 2) people who have trouble controlling their spending and would risk blowing their entire jackpot in a few short years.

Step 5: Select a financial coach Most people, except some people who have devoted their lives to personal finance, will need a financial coach in their corner giving them education, advice, and guidance in managing a sum of money that is far beyond what they previously contemplated having before they won the lottery. In selecting a financial coach, the three most important factors to consider are: 1) Fit, 2) education and expertise; and 3) costs.

Fit - Spend some time talking with your prospective financial coach about your financial situation and concerns. Ask what the coach would do. Share personal details. Get an understanding of the coach's personality and method of coaching. Then ask yourself if you would feel comfortable taking advice from that coach. Ask yourself if you will feel comfortable sharing your financial concerns and thoughts on an ongoing basis-- even after you make a dumb financial life move (it happens). Finally ask yourself if you could listen and follow through on the coach's advice even after she tells you that you made a dumb financial life move. You need a coach that you will listen to and allow to influence your financial decisions.

Education and Experience - You want to be confident that your financial coach knows what she is talking about. Ask how long the coach has been coaching. Ask how they developed their personal finance education and knowledge. Maybe the coach has written books, magazine articles, and speeches. Maybe the coach was highly recommended by someone you trust. However you decide, make sure there is some substance behind the relationship you will build with your financial coach.

Costs - Sure, you've become a rich person with your lottery winnings. However, that doesn't mean you can afford to ignore your expenses. The costs for a financial coach, especially a financial products salesperson masquerading as a financial coach, can be very high. You need to select a financial coach that can explain to you exactly how much her services cost. Your financial coach should also agree to not accept commissions from sellers of financial products. If a financial coach is receiving commissions when you buy financial products from her, you'll never know for sure whether the coach recommended you buy the product because of the commission or because the purchase is in your best interest.

Step 6: Work with Your Financial Coach Your financial coach can help you figure out how to pay for all of the things that are important to you (e.g. college for your kids, financial help for disadvantaged relatives), and create a lifetime allowance for you with something left over. You need to share all of your financial information and financial goals with the coach. Then you need to shut up and listen. Finally, you need to implement the advice of the coach. If you are not planning on implementing the coach's advice, say so. The coach will then work with you to develop an alternate financial plan that is more acceptable to you.

Step 7: Get Educated about Wealth and Stay Informed about Your Finances You need to know what is going on with your money. You can't outsource it all and just count on your coach to make sure money is magically available whenever you want to spend it. People that choose to stay in the dark and not pay attention to their personal finances generally end up not having any personal finances to pay attention to.

Chapter 5 - How Do You Rate?

As I write this we are well into election season. And everyone is promising to help the "middle class" without saying what they think the middle class is. I'd say about 90% of my friends and acquaintances identify themselves as part of the middle class; and 90% of the remainder identify themselves as part of the "upper middle class". That social class identification among the circle of people I interact with has been relatively constant throughout my adult life, and until recently I thought my social circle was representative of the population as a whole. In other words I thought that most people thought of themselves as middle class even though most people clearly are not.

Recently I read a survey conducted by the Gallup organization proving that my social circle is not representative of the population as a whole. In 2015 roughly half-- 51%-- of Americans identify as middle or upper middle class. 48% identify as "working class" or "lower class". Only 3% identify as "upper class". However, the survey doesn't actually define the incomes associated with these social classes.

While there is no official definition of middle class-- middle class is in the eye of the beholder. The often cited Pew Research Group defines the middle class as households with incomes between 2/3 and 2 times the median household income. For most parts of the country, that is somewhere between $55K and $150K for a family of 4. This definition considers only income as does not consider the age of the income earners, assets or debts. To me, a $100,000 per year family with $400K in mortgage and student loan debts and is only 5 years away from retirement should probably not consider themselves part of the middle class. While a $100,000 per year single person with a paid for house and is 25 years away from retirement is probably part of the upper class.

Middle class is really a state of mind, a feeling of relative comfort. To me, middle class is the feeling of being able to live a relatively comfortable lifestyle with a little bit left over every month. But if you want to know the actual "middle" in the US, it is about $53K per household. If your household income is far away from that number, it will be hard for you to claim you are middle class.

Many people are constantly seeking to scorecard their incomes against America as a whole. They want to know if they are in the 1% of top earners, 5%, 10% or whatever. The thing is, there is no one American experience, there is no one "Average American". It isn't reasonable to assume there is one income distribution. Incomes differ by age, race, gender, education level, and geography. Each family has different expense levels that can influence their financial lifestyle compared to their peers. Finally, some households benefit from having a significant net worth that can directly and indirectly contribute to their lifestyle.

Nonetheless, you want to know where you stand. I've been interested in the answer to that question for myself for some time. During my research for the writing of this chapter I've spent some time wondering why knowing my wealth ranking was so important to me, and many of the people I've talked to. The reason is that your wealth ranking is almost always higher than you think and feel it is based on your observations of those around you. Or, saying it in the reverse, you probably feel poorer than you actually are.

The cause of this phenomenon is both sociological and mathematical. In the US we are experiencing an ever growing income inequality (for the past 40 years), and a more recently growing social segregation (beginning around the dawn of Facebook). Social segregation occurs when your circle of friends, acquaintances, and influencers become increasingly homogenous across all social characteristics-- religion, politics, social status, wealth characteristics, family statuts, etc. In the age of Facebook it's become really easy to find and interact with like minded people and also really easy to distance yourself from people different from you. ("I don't like your offensive Facebook political rant-- 'UNFRIEND'; this political commentary is funny and insightful-- 'FRIEND REQUEST'.) So your friends are very likely to be in an income percentile very close to yours.

Income inequality is the catchphrase used to prove that a disproportionate share of the national income is being given to those at the top of the income scale. Income inequality also describes a mathematical distribution where there are lots of people with similar incomes at the low end, and then the income differential to the next percentage point up the income scale gets increasingly large.

Combining the effects of social segregation of income inequality means you are primarily exposed to people of a similar social class status as you. It also means that even if your income is in the middle of all your friends, your friends that are wealthier than you will be a lot wealthier, while your friends that are poorer than you will only be a little bit poorer. You'll be closer to the bottom income of your friends than the top. This makes you feel poorer than you actually are.

As an example, let's say your income is in the 80th percentile (about $100K/yr.) Your friends are most likely to be in a similar percentile. Possibly the 78th, 79th, 81st, and 82nd all in equal proportions. While that appears to put you in the middle income for your social group. However, the spread of your friends' incomes is likely to be $90K, $93K, $100K (you), $110K, and $125K. You are likely to feel relatively poor because your income is only $10K above your poorest friend, while it is $25K below your richest friend.

Interestingly, this phenomena holds for everyone all the way up the income scale. Take your $125K friend.

The incomes of the people in his social circle will also be skewed and may look something like this: $100K (you), $110K (a mutual friend), $125K, $150K, $185K. Your richest friend will also feel relatively poor because his income is closer to yours ($25K more) than it is to his richest friend ($60K less).

Now I've spent this entire chapter trying to convince you not to care how you rate, not to care what your income is relative to everyone else's. However you still do care, right? For some reason I do too.

Using CNN's analysis of 2015 household income data as a source, I present the following chart for you. Once you look at it and find out your income ranking, forget about it and stop worrying about your ranking so much.

Income Percentile	Household Income
Top 1%	$450K
Top 2%	$340K
Top 5%	$210K
Top 10%	$155K
Top 20%	$111K
Top 30%	$86K
Top 40%	$69K
Top 50%	$55K

Chapter 6 - Investing Personalities

Most people have a similar goal with regard to their personal finances. They want to maximize their ability to spend in retirement. Typically they want to achieve that with as little risk as possible. When I think of all the investing styles and personalities out there, almost all are suboptimal with respect to this goal. Here are a few of the common investing personalities I have run across.

Money is Burning a Hole In My Pocket
There are some people that can't seem to save a cent no matter how much money they have. Once they find out they are getting a bonus, they spend the money before the bonus check even lands in their hand. Every windfall seems just in time to pay for a much deserved and overdue treat. No matter how much money these people get, it's never enough. People in this group are never getting ahead, but always seeming to just get by.

Actually these people are in much worse shape than they appear to be because they don't have the financial standing to endure any financial adversity. And everyone experiences that eventually-- job loss, medical bill, unexpected car repair. Any one of these relatively common life events can send these people down the road to financial ruin. It can lead to running up a high interest credit card debt that they are unable to recover from, repossession, or even bankruptcy. Building a decent financial reputation and nest egg takes a long time. Nobody should do anything to risk having to start this process over.

People who are in this category have a reputation for lacking willpower when it comes to saving money. I have found, more often than not, that willpower isn't the issue for people in this category; the issue for them is they don't see a benefit to saving money. They spend all of their money on things that give them pleasure rather than saving money which they believe will give them no pleasure at all (because they ignore the future). Actually, it's a very rational choice given that fact pattern.

Financial plans won't remedy the behavior of these people because financial plans are formula and numbers based and target a particular wealth level that doesn't generate any pleasure. A more successful approach for this personality type is to envision the inevitable financial adversity that periodically comes your way. Envision it occurring one year from today. Now envision the financial disaster that will unfold if you continue on your current spending path. Contrast that vision with a second vision where the same financial adversity hits you in a year, but you have spent the year saving money, a vision where you can handle all or most of the adversity by writing a check. That second vision will be able to demonstrate in a concrete way the benefit of not spending all the money you have access to. This vision will be able to demonstrate that the benefit will come relatively quickly-- as soon as a year from now.

I Don't Want to Lose Any Money

My mom was in this category. She believed in investing, she just felt that it was unacceptable to lose any money at all. So in other words, she didn't believe in investing. She wanted a "sure thing". And we all know, there's no such thing as a "sure thing". So she was looking for an opportunity that didn't exist and as a result she had a hard time making financial decisions.

Investing involves risk. With every investment there is a chance you can lose money. With some investments there is a chance you can lose all of your money. This chance of losing money is what makes the investment great. You see, when there is a chance of losing money some potential investors will walk away from the investment and the price of the investment will have to decrease to attract enough buyers. As the purchase price of an investment goes down, the return increases, and that's what generates wealth for you.

In the real world, there are a few products that are called "risk free investments". They are pretty much limited to government bonds and CDs. At the time of this writing (Fall, 2017) high yielding CDs are paying approximately 1.25% per year before taxes, or about 0.93% after taxes. Inflation is running at about 1.70% (before and after taxes). Since inflation is higher than the after tax return of these investments, it means that these investments are guaranteed to lose money. Any financial product that is guaranteed to lose money can not be called an investment.

In order to generate favorable returns, you must accept some risk, and occasionally lose money in order for your investment dollars to keep up with inflation. If you fail to acknowledge that and hold on to your money too tightly, it will slowly slip away.

I Invest in Ideas
There are some people out there who only want to invest in ideas. They can tell you stories all day long about people who invested in ideas and then became billionaires. Then they go further and state that anyone who spends their time working for others is a sucker making someone else rich. A site called Quora.com where I answer people's financial questions is filled with people who recommend that you invest in ideas.

The thing about ideas is that ideas don't make any money at all. Companies successfully executing good ideas make money (sometimes). Everyone has great ideas. These ideas are worthless on their own. Most of these great ideas will stay ideas and never be acted on because people are often too lazy or scared to act on their ideas. Most of the people that use this investment philosophy use it to justify making investments without running all the numbers to see if the investment will ever lead to a profit.

Instead of focusing all their money on high risk ideas, people should put the majority of their investment dollars in proven ideas. Proven ideas can be found underlying investments in any publicly traded company. Most of your money should be invested in proven ideas. Then with a small portion of your investment dollars, invest in your own idea if you wish. This way you get exposure to the potential billion dollar payout from your great idea while still ensuring your investment portfolio will stay on track if the idea doesn't pan out.

Invest in Family
We all want to take care of family. However, it is important to distinguish "taking care of" family with "investing in family". Definitely run the numbers to see if the potential return relative to the risk of the investment is as good as you can get elsewhere. If it is, you are truly investing in family. Usually the potential return is poor, and your "investment" should be viewed as helping out family. I'm not saying not to help out your family, I'm encouraging you to be aware that your help is not an investment, and you should make sure you can afford to give this help.

I Prefer Exotic Investments
There's a lot of talk about how the poor's lack of financial education and power leads to their being targeted of by producers of overpriced, highly risky, low returning financial products. Some people conclude that they should focus on investing in what

the rich people invest in to immunize them from being taken advantage of.

Let me clue you in on a little secret-- middle class, rich people, and ultra rich people are all targeted. Financial scam artists are completely unbiased. All they care about is taking your money.

There are many terrible financial products that are sold to their customers by appealing to the vanity and ego of being associated with a product only available to the rich. Take hedge funds as an example. Because of the minimum deposit and net worth requirements, these funds are only available to the rich. In addition, many hedge funds make themselves even more exclusive by opening themselves to investment by invitation only. This exclusiveness can lead to investors becoming so desirous of a particular hedge fund that they ignore the quality of the investment. The truth is that most hedge funds have very high expenses and they have highly restrictive rules about when shares in the fund can be traded.

The typical hedge fund charges "two and twenty". This is shorthand for a 2% charge right off the top that never gets invested, and an annual charge of 20% of the profit. So, if you offered to invest $100K in a hedge fund and it returned 10% the following year, the hedge fund would invest $98K of your money, and then at the end of the year take $1960 of your return. You would be left with a balance of $105,840; if you instead invested the $100K in a low cost index fund and it also returned 10%, your balance would be somewhere around $109,900. The return on the hedge fund is slightly over half of the return of the low cost non-exclusive index fund.

Variable life, and some annuity products that are marketed to the upper middle class also have similar high expense characteristics.

There is no shortcut to ensuring that you are making a sound financial investment. You have to do your homework on every investment opportunity no matter what the product is, who it is marketed to, or what company is selling it. You have to make sure your money will work as hard as possible because nobody else will do that for you.

Trading System
Sometimes people spend some time seeing patterns and can't miss systems in the market that aren't there. Here's the thing: there is so much data, so many places to look for patterns that you are bound to find one. Except it isn't a pattern, it is a coincidence. A coincidence that will likely not be repeated going forward. You absolutely should not invest based on a coincidence.

It's very easy to distinguish a pattern from a coincidence. You can explain why a pattern should occur. You can't explain why a coincidence should occur. It just happened due to random luck.

Now patterns are something that are worthwhile knowing about. If you know about a reliable stock market pattern, that knowledge should enable you profit going forward. However, it is unlikely you will ever find a reliable pattern that can help you increase your investment performance. One of the billion other people and computers analyzing stock market charts would have found it before you.

So let go of the idea that there is a surefire get rich quick trading algorithm. It's just not going to happen. Get back to buy and hold investing for the long term. That's where the money is at.

My Labor Doesn't Cost Anything, So My Investments Use a Lot of My Labor

I've seen lots of people purchase or develop a business that they find to be very profitable. They are quite satisfied with the profit it generates and are pleased with its return on investment. Often they are so happy with its performance as an investment that they are willing to spend a significant amount of time working on the business, improving it, and enhancing its profitability. They use the fact that the business generates a favorable return to justify the time spent on the business.

But here's the thing, the value of the work you spend on the business must be considered a business expense before you compare its return with the return of other investments. Most investments do not require any work at all. Comparing the return of a business that requires a significant amount of your labor with the return of an investment that requires no labor at all is not a fair comparison.

First, ask yourself how much would you have to pay someone else to perform the labor you are performing for your business? Second, you can reduce that cost by the business expense tax deduction you would receive if you paid someone else. The tax deduction is equal to your marginal tax rate times the business expense. For example, if you would have to pay someone $50 to mow the lawn at a house you rent out, your net business expense cost is $50 - 25% x $50 = $37.50. This net business expense should be reduced from the profit you calculate for your business. Make sure to include all of your labor including the value of the executive decisions you make for your business, your effort in generating sales, and all of the behind the scenes bookkeeping and paperwork you have to perform.

If your efforts in managing your business is reducing your ability to earn paying work, then the value of your labor is at least as much as your after - tax lost wages.

Often many side businesses turn out to be very poor investments once personal labor is properly valued. Go through the effort of adjusting your calculation of business profitability for the expense of your labor and see if your business is truly as profitable as you think it is.

Chapter 7 - Sources of Investing Information

Often when a person starts down the road of committing to doing what it takes to build a secure financial future, they also commit to educating themselves about personal finance. They want to know how to invest their growing financial nest egg and make the financial decisions necessary to keep the secure financial future on track.

Throughout this book we have traced how the financial decisions and issues change as your wealth grows from $1000 to $10,000 to $100,000 to $1,000,000 and beyond. Your personal finance knowledge must grow as well if you wish to stay on top of your finances. Although ultimately I became formally educated in personal finance by taking a two year Certified Financial Planner certificate program and completed several of the examinations offered by credentialing agencies. Most of my personal finance education was outside of the classroom. I pursued this education out of interest in the topic and a need to manage my net worth as it grew. Here's how I did just that.

Late Teens - Early Adulthood
Most people have little or no money in this stage of their lives. Even the thought of saving for a car purchase four years away can feel like forever. However, at this stage in your financial lives, building investment knowledge should take a back burner to

cash flow management. You have lots of opportunity to learn all about cash flow management.

First, start with your own cash flow. Start tracking it. If you want to be fancy, buy a copy of Quicken or use an online source like Mint. These are applications that allow you to track all of your income and expenses, assets and liabilities, and cash flow in one place. These apps do more than just balance your checkbook. These apps easily answer questions like, "how much did I spend on entertainment last month," or "what will my bank balance be in six months?"

Some of your finances may already by online if you have an online bank account. These accounts will let you download transactions directly into Quicken in order to save you time. To the extent that your personal finances are handled in cash, you can and should track that too. Especially if cash transactions are a significant part of your spending. The idea here is to document where all your money came from and where it goes. Once you have done that for a couple of months, you will begin to develop a great understanding of your current spending. This understanding will make you think more about your spending and eliminate all of the wasteful spending you engage in that doesn't contribute to your happiness.

A next idea is to enlist your parents in your education. Offer to help them with managing their finances. You can balance their checkbook. If they aren't already tracking their finances, you can get them started on

Quicken. As you are doing that, you can learn how they are managing their cash flow. You will also get a great feel for how much "real life" costs. Additionally, if your family is like many others, the family will be filling out the FAFSA form (college financial aid form). Enlist yourself in helping your parents prepare the form. This form contains very detailed information of your family's income and expenses. Go over the form with your parents and discuss it with them. Ask them about any items on the financials that surprise you. If your parents have never shared their personal financial information with you, then there are bound to be some surpirses. Another great source of education about your family's finances is your parents' tax returns and pay stubs. These are all great real world foundations for educational discussions about personal finance with people who have been managing personal finance issues for a few decades.

Hopefully your parents' need for personal finance secrecy won't inhibit this valuable education. If they do resist, share with them that your goal is to be educated about personal finance and benefit from the wisdom of their experience. They will likely come around at that point because they want to make sure you don't experience financial ruin and come back home to live on their sofa in a few years.

As you are preparing to enter the career of your choice, make sure you get an understanding of what your income will be starting out. Go online to a paycheck calculator to calculate your monthly take home pay. Now prepare a budget based on that take home pay. Make sure you include about 10% - 15% of your take home for emergencies and retirement. Make sure you feel comfortable with the lifestyle you will have if you follow that budget. If the lifestyle arising from your budget seems too frugal then you have two choices: 1) identify a higher paying job available to you that you can enjoy, or 2) adjust your lifestyle expectations downward. You must choose one or your are going to begin you adult life "in the hole" and possibly never dig your way out.

Beginning of Career

Once your formal education is over and you begin having actual money to handle, it's time to develop a broad general financial education. For starters, regularly read personal finance publications-- *Money* and *Kiplingers' Personal Finance* are two great monthly publications that are well suited for people at the beginning of their careers. These publications cover a wide variety of topics that are relevant to middle to upper income individuals. They address personal finance issues from all angles -- income maximization, investment gain maximization, tax reduction, and expense reduction. Read the entire magazine even if a topic doesn't seem relevant. The topic may become relevant some day in the future. The only part of these publications that are of questionable value is the part that makes forecasts of the performance of particular stocks. These publications regularly put out articles with titles like "6 Stocks to Buy Now", and "7 Stocks for the Long

Term". These articles are generally worthless and provide stock picks that perform no better than the proverbial monkey throwing darts at the stock pages. It is not in your best interest to make changes to your personal financial situation based on these articles alone.

The *Wall Street Journal* is also worth a look every once in a while. Most of that paper deals with corporate finance and issues relevant to corporate senior management. However, there is a decent portion of content (about 20%) that is related to personal finance.

Thirdly, you may want to enlist a financial coach in helping you. This can happen if your income and complexity of your personal finance situation grows faster than the knowledge you are developing.

In addition, keep the option of hiring a financial coach in mind whenever you could use input from an expert in personal finance to keep you on track.

Mid Career and Beyond
By this time, your financial education may be broad enough to keep you from making any major mistakes. Your financial situation is also more complex. Here you need to develop a more targeted approach to personal finance education. As you identify an area of personal finance you must address, you can go out and seek information on that specific topic. The answer to any personal finance question is only a search engine away. Also continue to follow personal

finance news through your favorite finance publication or blog (like www.typezfinance.com).

At times you may want to check in with a financial coach (like me at ForwardFinancial Planners.com) if you have a particularly challenging issue or you have a personal finance decision to make that is potentially worth more that the fee of the financial coach.

Chapter 8 - Cautionary Tales

Most people I know are burying their head in the sand and pretending they are in good financial shape for retirement. It's easy to do that because retirement doesn't cost anything today. However, every dollar you don't spend on retirement investments today will require you to spend two dollars on retirement investments in ten years. The reason for that is that your retirement money invested today will approximately double every ten years. If you choose not to make your retirement contribution today, you'll have to come up with twice as much money ten years down the line. You can and should think of it as a retirement savings sale with a ptichman screaming at you on late night TV: "50% off if you save today!", "prices will never be lower", "Prices will double in ten years!" "You can't afford to wait!".

Some people may feel that retirement savings isn't something to worry about. They work hard and will collect Social Security. They may also be one of the fortunate 11% of all workers under 30 who will become eligible for a pension when they retire. The combination of social security and a pension go a long way towards delivering a retirement income to replace your working income. Unfortunately they don't go all the way. Even if you are eligible for both Social Security and a pension, you will still have to save for retirement to supplement those two income sources.

The average social security check is about $1020 per month (as of 2014) for those over 65. The maximum social security check, which is paid to earners who have earned $115K+ (inflation adjusted) for 35 or more years, is about $2600 per month. High earners can push that monthly check up to $3000 per month if they are willing to wait until age 70 to begin collecting.

Pension benefits are also not as generous as many people believe. At a high level, pension benefits are computed by a formula related to 3 items: 1) years of service at your employer; 2) average monthly pay; 3) pension factor (typically between 1.5% and 2.0%). So as an example, let's say you earned $100K per year at an employer for 20 years; and let's say that employer offered a pension with a pension factor of 1.6%. Your pension benefit would be $100K x 20 x 1.6% = $32K per year or $2666 per month. Most people who receive pension benefits receive a much smaller pension because it is unusual to stay at the same employer for 20 years. It goes without saying that if you were at that employer for 10 years (still a long time), your pension would be half what was computed above - $1,333 per month.

So, best case scenario, you receive $2600 / month from social security and another $2666 from a pension for a total of $5266 per month or $63,192 per year. In retirement you are getting a pay cut of at least 37% from your working pay of $115K+. Even this person experiencing the best case scenario will need to save for retirement.

Most of us won't be getting a pension, and will experience a much deeper pay cut than 37% unless we save, and save big. How big? About 25 years of the spending you need on top of Social Security. As an example, let's say you currently live on a $50K per year income and want to be able to spend $35K per year in retirement. You went to the Social Security Website (www.ssa.gov) and learned that your social security benefit will be $15K per year. You'll need $20K extra per year to live your desired lifestyle in retirement. That will require a $500K retirement nest egg. On top of that Fidelity Investments and other organizations estimate that a retired couple will have out of pocket medical costs in retirement of $250K. While a $750K total retirement savings need sounds huge, if you begin early, you can get there for as little as 10% of your income, or a 4 hour a week side job. However, if you wait until you are in your mid 40's to start thinking aobut retirement, you'll have to save 3 times as much per paycheck to get to the same spot. Retirement savings is not something you can ignore.

Chapter 9 - Charity

Charitable giving is obviously an optional part of personal finance. This chapter will not be about tithing or encouraging others to accept a moral or religious obligation to be charitable. Instead it is about smart ways to be charitable and doing the most good with the money you choose to be charitable with.

In the last chapter I will share my mother's story as an inspiring tale on investing. I described the story about creating and discussing a budget with her. During that discussion I also mentioned charity. I said something like "you need to contribute to charity. The average person contributes 3% of their income to charity every year." My mother couldn't make ends meet as it was. She responded very simply with "I'M A CHARITY!!!"

You see, she felt the best way she could do good in the world was to invest in her family. She enabled me to earn an income, support my child's future, pay for retirement, and still have money left over. I, my son, and all future generations will be able to be charitable far beyond what my mother could have delivered.

So my first guidance on charity is don't be charitable with your money until you have secured your own personal financial situation. Think of this guidance like the airplane safety precaution "In case of emergency, air masks will drop from the ceiling. Please put on your own mask before helping others.". There's no sense in donating to a charity if it puts you at risk of needing to receive charitable assistance at some point in the future.

That means that people donating to charity while carrying significant credit card debt are doing something completely irrational. Why would anyone donate $1000 to charity today and pay their credit card company an additional $200 in interest payments to do so when they could use the $1000 to pay down their credit card debt and have a $200 savings on interest payments per year which they could use for charitable giving? I believe any charity would rather receive $200 per year beginning next year over receiving $1000 today and nothing in the future. In my view, taking control of your personal finances and maximizing your net worth is being charitable because it allows you to increase your charitable donations in the future. That's why you should wait until you are set for life until you focus on being charitable.

Easy to say, but you may feel that you will never be set for life. You're wrong. It costs nothing to die so the moment before your death, you are set for life. While it's not possible to make significant donations to charity immediately before you die, it's very easy to make lots of donations after you die. You can put a provision for charity in your will. You can choose a specific dollar amount, a percentage of your net worth, or specific assets (like your house or car). Read the chapter on wills earlier in this book for more on how to do that.

Formula
The need for charitable giving in this world is essentially infinite. Every charity always needs more money for their good works. Deciding to give charitably whenever you see the need will bankrupt even the wealthiest philanthropist. On the other hand, giving to charity negatively impacts your and / or your heirs net worth. Intentionally harming your own net worth goes against all the lessons of personal finance.

I believe the best way to move away from those two suboptimal outcomes is to create an objective methodology to determine the amount you will give to charity. Tithing is an obvious example. It is simple and objective. There are other systems that can work too. You should select a system that objectively decides when you can contribute to charity and what amount you can contribute. Tithing is one based only on income. You can incorporate lots of considerations into your system. For example, my system considers the number of people in our household. Once my son moves out, our charitable donations are likely to increase.

Smart and Efficient Ways to Give
Of course you should make sure that the charity you donate to is helping causes that are worthwhile to you. But that's not enough. There are lots of charities supporting worthwhile causes. Some are much more efficient than others. Efficiency for a charity means that it uses most of its money on the cause it supports

and very little of its money on administration, fundraising, executive salaries, and other corporate expenses. The most efficient charities are 80% or more efficient meaning $80 out of every $100 you donate will go to those in need. Some terrible charities are less than 10% efficient. All things being equal, you want your charitable donations to go to a charity that is more efficient. You can find out the efficiency rating of a charity by asking the charity for its financial information. Or you can go online to one of several services that rate charities according to this metric. One of the most popular is CharityNavigator.com

Tax Benefits
Once you've determined the charity and amount you wish to give, you want to give in the smartest way possible that maximizes the benefit to the charity and minimizes the effect of the donation on your net worth. People have written entire books on how to maximize the tax benefit of charitable donations. There are many strategies and some are quite complex, especially for the super wealthy (net worth above $5 million).

Here I focus on more basic strategies that target the remaining 99% or so of the population.

First, and most obvious, is for you to get a valid receipt for your charitable donation. If you are donating items of value, they must be valued as the current market value (i.e. what you can sell the item for) rather than what you paid for it when it was newer. If you are donating money, the value of the donation equals the amount of the donation minus the value of anything you got in return. For example if you paid $100 for a charity dinner, the value of your charitable donation equals $100 minus the value of the dinner. If you are donating investments, the value of your donation is the market value of the investment.

The value of any charitable donation you have is a tax deduction for those who itemize their taxes. There is a "Standard Deduction" of $6,300 for single people and $12,600 for married people. If your tax deductions total more than this amount in a year, you should be itemizing your deductions.

Tip #1: Donate more to charity in years where you itemize your deductions.

The value of your donation reduces your taxable income. As a result, your donation will reduce your taxes by the amount of your donation times your tax bracket. So charitable donations reduce your taxes more in years where you are in a higher tax bracket.

Tip #2: Donate more to charity in years where you are in a higher tax bracket.

For people who don't have an investment portfolio, tips #1 and #2 are about the best you can do in managing your tax burden related to charitable contributions. For those that do have an investment portfolio, read on.

Investment gains are not taxed until they are sold. The law allows you to transfer investments directly to a charity. You don't have to sell the investment first, and then send a check. What this means is that you can legally avoid ever paying capital gains tax on your investment if you transfer it directly to a charity. You do this by filling out a form with your broker instructing a direct transfer to the charity's brokerage account (call the charity to find this information). You never take possession of the investment proceeds. The charity receives the investment and sells it immediately. They send you a letter informing you of the dollars they received from your investment. This letter serves as a receipt and a valuation of your tax deduction. If you still believe in the investment for the long term, you can wait 30 days and then buy the investment again with your cash on hand. When you sell the investment for real some day in the future, your capital gain will be based on this new, higher purchase price. You will never have to pay capital gains tax on the investment gain from the day you originally purchased the investment to the day you transferred the investment to the charity.

By transferring an investment to a charity, you reduce your taxes in two ways. First, you get the same tax deduction as you would if you donated cash. Second, you pay less capital gains tax in the future whenever you do decide to sell the investment.

For example, let's say you want to donate $2000 to the charity of your choice. You have a stock that you bought for $1000 three years ago that is now worth $2000. Call your broker, and instruct the broker to transfer the stock to the charity. The charity will sell the stock for $2000 and send you a receipt. This will be one of the itemized deductions on your tax return. If you are in the 28% tax bracket, your income tax this year will go down by $560. In thirty days you buy back the stock for $2000. The stock price doesn't move and eventually you choose to sell it for $2000. Since there was no gain after you repurchased the stock, there will be no capital gains tax. If you had kept the original shares purchased for $1000, there would have been a $1000 gain on the sale, and your capital gains tax would have been $150. This charitable contribution of $2000 saved you a total of $710 in taxes. Fantastic! That's $710 more for you or $710 more than you can contribute to charity in the future.

Tip #3: If you can, transfer highly appreciated investments to charity rather than donating cash.

The last tip is for people over 70 1/2. People in this age group are required to receive distributions from their Traditional IRAs every year. These distributions are taxable as income. Remember, you don't pay tax when you contribute to the Traditional IRA. When you take the money out, you do have to pay.

There is one exception, though. You can direct the IRA custodian to transfer your distribution directly to a charity. The money delivered straight to the charity doesn't count as income at all. You get to avoid the taxes you would have paid on the distribution. In this scenario, you don't have to worry about itemizing deductions or the limits on charitable contributions. Instead the tax benefit comes from avoiding the income tax on your IRA distribution. There are situations where it more advantageous to transfer investments to charity than this approach. Please ask a tax expert to run the numbers for your specific situation before you take action.

Tip #4: If you are getting retirement distributions from an IRA and you don't itemize deductions, transfer your IRA distribution directly to the charity.

The goal of this chapter is to give you some information that will help you deliver the most good for your charitable dollar. Also, you must remember that the first step in being charitable is to make sure your own financial situation is in order.

Chapter 10 - An Inspiring Tale - Rags to Riches

I want to inspire rather than scare you into making the effort to take control of your personal finances. And I know that in order to be inspired, two things have to happen. First, you must feel confident that you can succeed. This book aims to give you that confidence. Taking control of your personal finances is not that hard, and the book gives an overview on how to handle all of the common personal finance milestones people experience in life. I hope that when you reach each of these milestones, you use the working knowledge that you developed from reading the book. That working knowledge is enough for you to "know what you don't know" about your specific situation. You can then gather the additional information you need through additional research and / or engaging a financial coach to make an informed decision. Did I tell you that I am a financial coach? My tagline is "Never make an Uninformed Financial Decision Again".

Confidence in the ability to succeed isn't enough to inspire you to take action. I am confident that I could memorize pi to 100 decimal places if I set my mind to it. But I am never going to do that. I just don't see that as fun or worthwhile. In order to be inspired to take action, you must feel the action is worth the effort. The goal of this chapter is to convince you that your effort to take control of your finances is worthwhile. My mother's financial story should do the trick.

My Mother

My mother grew up as one of thirteen kids on a remote farm on the Plains of Saskatchewan. She definitely did not receive an education in personal finance. As you might have already guessed she did receive an education in the school of hard work.

Fast forwarding a few decades... My mother was a single parent in The Bronx, New York City with credit card debt and a net worth of less than zero. She wanted life to be easier both for her and me. She certainly had the ability to work hard; and she certainly knew that financial security was worth the effort. At that time she was over 40 years old and had experienced financial insecurity every day of her life. But she still didn't have any knowledge of personal finance.

Her first move to deliver financial security to the family (the two of us) was really an investment decision. She saw that I was achieving the intellectual milestones at a younger age than other little kids. She felt that we could use that as a ticket to a financially secure life. She asked around to find the "best school in New York", contacted them, and asked the school to admit me. I was five years old.

There were a couple of problems with that. For one, she hadn't filled out an application and the deadline had passed. She didn't even know that schools required an application. More significantly, though, the school was for the wealthy. The tuition at the time was significant and approaching half of her income. She could barely make ends meet without a tuition payment. That school wasn't for me.

Well, my mother kept pressing our case. We ended up meeting with the principal of the Nursery School at her house. Apparently we impressed, somewhat. The school offered her a tuition discount that would require her to pay "only" 20% to 25% of her take home pay. She agreed. I was in the best, most expensive school in New York. The school of Rockefellers. My mother continued to pay 20% to 25% of her income to the school all the way until I graduated high school thirteen years later. That's what you would call a nontraditional investment-- it was illiquid and had a very far off time for the investment to pay off. My mother was "all in" on this investment. Her net worth outside of her investment in me remained less than zero until late in my high school years when she was over 50 years old.

During middle school I began to be interested in personal finance issues primarily because we were living a financially insecure life where "I can't afford it," was a daily tagline. I didn't want to live life like that. I learned about budgeting and offered to prepare a budget for my mom. She agreed. After all of her regular bills and our food, there were exactly $11 per month left over for everything else-- clothing, entertainment, toys, doctors, etc. I observed from the budget that my mother was not contributing anything towards retirement savings. When I told her she should be saving for retirement, she responded "You are my retirement plan"!

Ultimately I moved on to a successful professional life. I estimate that my schooling set me on a path to earn roughly double what I would have earned if my mother hadn't made that investment. Over the course of my career my increased earnings from her investment will be in the millions.

My mother's attention to long-term thinking, conservative spending, and planning for the future has brought me to the financially secure life that my family has today. Like my mother, I also have invested in my son's education. However, unlike her, I didn't have to sacrifice all of the cash flow from my son's childhood to make that investment happen. We don't live in perpetual financial insecurity. I have my own retirement plan. My son will not experience the burden of being financially responsible for me. His financial life is his own.

While my mother didn't get to see the full reward of her investment, I did. The full reward of her investment came two generations later. She gave the grandson she never met a financially comfortable childhood.

www.ingramcontent.com/pod-product-compliance
Lightning Source LLC
Chambersburg PA
CBHW070237230526
45470CB00002B/446